CRESTWOOD PUBLIC LIBRARY

W9-BEU-889

Praise for *101 Best Ways to Land a Job in Troubled Times*

"A true A-to-Z approach to landing the job of your choice regardless of market conditions. Jay's book empowers job seekers to take control of their future by being proactive, resourceful, and innovative—including building a referral network both online and off. If you are serious about landing a quality job quickly in today's job market, this book will practically guarantee your success."

Bob Burg
Author of Endless Referrals *and*
The Go-Giver

"Jay has written a unique and highly effective book combining motivational techniques with job search innovation. Jay offers fresh, exciting, and timely strategies, tools, and processes to help people land jobs in troubled times and in highly competitive job markets. This book is way overdue, is enjoyable and easy to read, and offers encouragement and specifics to successfully meet the challenges of today's troubling economy and job market. This is a must-read book for everyone seeking a new/better job."

Susan Leventhal
Manager, Professional Placement Network
Workforce One, South Florida

"Jay Block has taken his place as one of the career-coaching industry's most innovative thinkers and contributors. He is always challenging traditional ways of thinking to develop new techniques and tools to inspire people to achieve career and life success. *101 Best Ways to Land a Job in Troubled Times* is his very best work. Jay continues to find new and effective approaches to challenge us all to successfully navigate through these trouble economic times and secure meaningful and sustainable jobs."

Frank X. Fox
Executive Director, Professional Association of Résumé
Writers & Career Coaches

"This book is a must-read for all job seekers in today's highly competitive job market. Whether you're a graduating student or a transitional worker, you will benefit from all the simple motivational techniques and career management tips that are offered from cover to cover."

Sherry Zylka, MA
Associate Dean of Continuing Education and
Workforce Development
Schoolcraft College, Michigan

101
BEST WAYS
TO LAND
A JOB IN
TROUBLED TIMES

Other Titles from Jay Block

101 Best Resumes

101 Best Cover Letters

101 More Best Resumes

Great Questions! Great Answers! For Your Job Interview

202 Great Resumes

101 Best Resumes to Sell Yourself

2500 Keywords to Get You Hired

101 Best Resumes for Grads

101 Best Tech Resumes

101
BEST WAYS
TO LAND
A JOB IN
TROUBLED TIMES

JAY A. BLOCK

New York   Chicago   San Francisco   Lisbon   London
Madrid   Mexico City   Milan   New Delhi   San Juan
Seoul   Singapore   Sydney   Toronto

Crestwood Public
Library District
4955 W. 135th Street
Crestwood, IL 60445

650.14
BLO
2/11

*The **McGraw·Hill** Companies*

Copyright © 2010 by Jay A. Block. All rights reserved. Printed in the United States of America. Except as permitted under the United States Copyright Act of 1976, no part of this publication may be reproduced or distributed in any form or by any means, or stored in a data base or retrieval system, without the prior written permission of the publisher.

1 2 3 4 5 6 7 8 9 0   FGR/FGR   0 1 0 9

ISBN 978-0-07-166328-1
MHID   0-07-166328-2

Interior design by Ginger Graziano Design Group.

McGraw-Hill books are available at special quantity discounts to use as premiums and sales promotions, or for use in corporate training programs. To contact a representative, please e-mail us at bulksales@mcgraw-hill.com.

This book is printed on acid-free paper.

This book is dedicated to all you job seekers who have not given up on your dreams or settled for less than you can be.

CONTENTS

FOREWORD

Susan D. Corey, M.Ed., CEIP, CWDP, BES, MS
Southeast Michigan Community Alliance; Manager of Workforce Development
Board Member, The National Association of Workforce Development Professionals

Dear Reader:

Every once in a while you meet someone using his gifts and talents to really make a difference in people's lives. Jay Block is that person. His message is a clarion call for you to take action in your life: to provide a guide on how to survive and thrive not only in this troubled economy but when the good times return (and they will), and to motivate yourself to achieve all that you are capable of and deserve. Finally, someone provides an upbeat and inspirational approach to career management and job change! Jay combines commanding motivational techniques with a highly effective strategic process for making a successful and rewarding job change. He makes the process of pursuing and landing a new job fun and enjoyable. He shows you how to remain fearless, hopeful, confident, and engaged in the wake of adversity and setbacks. And his good news is that the process of landing a job in troubled times is simple. This book will show you just how simple. The only thing you need to do is work diligently at what is simple.

101 Best Ways to Land a Job in Troubled Times will be the only job transition resource you will need to land a new job or discover your true calling. Tough economic times and competitive job markets require new ways of thinking, new beliefs, enjoyable processes, and a renewed sense of hope. Jay is a pioneer in the career management industry, by definition, an innovative thinker. The foundation of his success—which he measures by the success of his clients—was built over the past 20 years by constantly applying new ways of thinking so you can better plan your career and achieve your career goals. Actually, this book is not only a book on job transition and career management, it is also a book on how to significantly improve your quality of life. You will be inspired to take specific actions that will lead to a "richer" life!

So, if you are ready to enrich your quality of your life and take control of your career, immerse yourself in the material Jay presents in this book. Cherish the time you spend working through the processes Jay introduces. Revel in the experience of approaching the entire job transition process with a whole new attitude and a whole new set of tools and strategies. And then watch your new future unfold!

Thank you, Jay, for sharing and caring!

PREFACE

I was fired by one of my best friends in 1992. More on this later. But first I want you to know that this book was written for you, and I want you to think of me as your personal coach, one who truly cares about you and your future … because I do! I have worked with thousands of people from around the world to help them identify, pursue, and secure well-paying jobs and rewarding opportunities in troubled economies. Though you and I, most likely, have not met formally, I fully understand and empathize with what you are currently experiencing and the emotional roller-coaster you are riding.

This book is different from most other job search books because I reject the idea that job search is an effective activity, or that it works at all. As you will see during our time together, *career and job transition is a process*, not a search. Whether you are a graduating student or seasoned professional, career and job transition can be compared to planning and orchestrating a political campaign. Politicians who seek to get "hired" for elected office do not conduct a political search; they conduct a strategic campaign. So must you. And once you embrace this new way of thinking, you will 1) have much more control over your future, 2) secure rewarding opportunities quickly at the pay you deserve, and 3) genuinely enjoy the process, in both favorable or troubled job markets!

I have worked with people who have been unexpectedly terminated, downsized, rightsized, and capsized. I have worked with those who have bosses from you-know-where, who are stressed out from working in toxic environments, and who are toiling every day at jobs that are downright uninspiring. Many clients and audiences that I have addressed over the past 20-plus years are still in "What do I want to be when I grow up?" mode. And yet others are hampered by golden handcuffs, tethered to an unexciting and taxing job. They are unable to seek out new opportunities because economic and financial considerations are such that they can't relinquish their current jobs and because they are so exhausted and stressed out at the end of the day, they haven't the energy to pursue better opportunities. Finally, I have worked with employees wanting to start their own enterprises as well as entrepreneurs wanting to convert to employees.

So I feel like I know you and the challenges you face. And you should know that we are kindred spirits. When I graduated from the University of New Hampshire in the mid-1970s, in the midst of a severe recession, the unemployment rate was near 8 percent. It took me months to find a management trainee job that paid just 10 cents over minimum wage! However, I accepted the job and worked my way up to an operations manager in just six months. Then, at age 26, I quit my job and started my own company and sold it for a handsome profit at age 30. I subsequently went into business in partnership with a French company and proceeded to lose just about everything by the time I was 31. I came close to bankruptcy. I continued to struggle to find my place in the labor market over the next seven years. Then, in 1991, one of my best friends hired me as his marketing director. A year later he fired me. Well, actually, he was conveniently out of town, so he had my secretary inform me that I was fired when I returned from my vacation. How many people are fired by their secretaries on orders from one of their best friends?

So there I was, 39 years old, broke and broken. I was broke financially. I was broken physically, 15 pounds out of shape. And, most critically, I was broken emotionally. I had lost my confidence, my dignity, and any hope for the future. I was forced to reinvent myself but had no idea how to do it. So I sought out and worked with some of the world's most reputable coaches, poured through more than 1,000 books and audiotapes, and, by the age of 45, found my passions, emerged as an industry leader, and became a well-respected author and national trainer. The point I am making is that I have experienced much of what you are experiencing. I've been there, done that, and worn that tee shirt. But I succeeded, as will you.

Since 1993, I have interviewed thousands of hiring managers, HR professionals, and executive recruiters to determine what they look for and what they want when they are hiring. Armed with this information, I discovered that most of what you've been taught about the job search makes no sense, is contrary to effective and accepted methods of marketing, and is an exercise filled with fear and anxiety, not excitement and anticipation. So I set out to identify a commonsense and motivational process that would successfully work for anyone ... and found it! Since then, I have assisted tens of thousands of people to clearly identify, pursue, and achieve meaningful jobs and career objectives.

So I invite you to spend some time with me so you too can achieve all that you deserve. In fact, I invite you to treat our time together as an *enjoyable journey* that will do for you what it did for me—give you confidence, self-respect, and genuine enthusiasm for creating a better future.

ACKNOWLEDGMENTS

I owe a debt of gratitude to literally hundreds and hundreds of people from around the globe over the past 20 years who have helped shape me as an industry professional. It would, no doubt, take up dozens of pages to name all of them, and I'm afraid I'd still omit many key names from that list. So to all those with whom I have had the pleasure and honor of sharing experiences over the past two decades, thank you for your friendships, contributions, and support.

This is my tenth book published by McGraw-Hill, which has shown itself to be a professional and highly supportive organization, and I am grateful that the company has given me the opportunity to work on books that help people support themselves and their families. This book is the most important one I have ever written, and a book that is sorely needed in these troubling economic times. *101 Best Ways to Land a Job in Troubled Times* is the only motivational career book of its kind. Indeed, most of us can use as much motivation as we can get.

I want to especially thank my editor, Ed Chupak, who went to bat for me in selling this book idea to McGraw-Hill. I am sure that without Ed's belief in the importance of a resource like this and in my ability to produce it at the level demanded by McGraw-Hill, this book would still be a dream in this author's heart and mind. I owe a debt to Mary Glenn, editorial director, and Philip Ruppel, president of McGraw-Hill Professional, who have supported my work over the past 12-plus years. And a special thank you to Janice Race, senior editing supervisor, who made the editing process not only bearable—but highly enjoyable. I also want to extend a very warm thank you to my copyeditor, Judy Duguid. She treated this manuscript as though it were her own, and I was, to say the least, more than impressed with her work. Overall, McGraw-Hill provided a support team that was, in a word, unequaled.

I want to thank the following industry professionals who provided insight and timely quotes for this book: Frank Fox, executive director of the Professional Association of Résumé Writers and Career Coaches; Kathryn Troutman, bestselling author of *10 Steps to a Federal Job*; Bob Burg, national bestselling author of *Endless Referrals*; Tim Best, principal and senior vice president for Bradley-Morris, Inc., the nation's premier career placement firm for veteran job placement; Sarah Hightower Hill, CEO of Chandler Hill Partners, a national outplacement firm; Andrew J. Tabone, manager, Information Systems, Recruitment and Career Development at Carnival Cruise Lines; Martin Buckland, a well-respected master career coach in Ontario, Canada; and Susan J. Cook, executive vice president and chief human resources officer, Eaton Corporation.

And a very special thank you to Susan D. Corey of the Southeast Michigan Community Alliance, manager of Workforce Development, and board member of the National Association of Workforce Development Professionals for writing the foreword to the book. My gratitude goes also to Susan Leventhal, PPN manager, Workforce One, South Florida, who has been a friend and professional colleague for over 20 years.

Finally, and most important, I want to thank my wife, Ellen, an executive career coach and attorney. Over and over again she proofread the manuscript before I submitted it to McGraw-Hill. She supported me in every aspect of writing this book, and she kept me on an even keel during the numerous times I almost capsized. Without her love and patience, guidance, and belief in this important work, I might not have survived this project, which had a very tight deadline. She was my rock and my greatest supporter throughout this project—as she is in my life.

Very few people, including employment professionals, ever analyze and appreciate the complexities of one of life's most necessary skills—getting a job. This book acknowledges those complexities and breaks them down into an easy five-step *process*. When you finish reading this book, you'll be well on your way to being proficient with all the complexities of getting a job … while enjoying the *process*!

Definition of a Job Seeker

A person who is seeking a job and who must be highly proficient at:

- Goal Setting
- Self-Analysis
- Writing
- Word Processing
- Marketing
- Networking
- Stress Management
- Interviewing

- Strategic Planning
- Market Analysis
- Editing
- The Internet
- Sales
- Time Management
- Overcoming Objections
- Negotiating

- Competitive Analysis
- Self-Motivation
- Proofreading
- Logistics
- Cold Calling
- Research
- Health and Fitness
- Decision Making

101
BEST WAYS
TO LAND
A JOB IN
TROUBLED TIMES

WHAT YOU NEED TO KNOW BEFORE WE START

HOW BELIEFS AFFECT OUTCOME

Most successful endeavors are a result of successful processes. There is a process we go through to graduate high school and college. There is a process for baking a cake, for writing a book, for conducting a marriage ceremony, and for building and managing a business enterprise. And there is a process for landing a well-paying, rewarding job as well. The challenge is that if you were to ask 25 employment experts what the process is, you'd get either a bunch of blank stares or 25 different, oftentimes conflicting, opinions. I would venture to guess that most would simply provide the same advice that has been circulating for about 70 years now; namely, put your résumé together and work on interviewing skills.

GOOD NEWS: THE PROCESS IS EASY!

The good news is that the process for landing a well-paying, rewarding job in both favorable and troubled economies is an easy five-step process. All you need to know is what the steps are and then master them. And this would be an appropriate time to dispel any idea that there is a magic pill that you can take to land that next best job. There isn't one. But the five-step process *is* easy; anyone can follow the steps successfully and enthusiastically.

You only have to work hard at what's easy. The reason why so many people struggle with their job search efforts is because they don't know the process or they don't follow it. Indeed, it is a proven, successful process that will work for anyone who commits to it.

THE STRANGEST SECRET

More than 40 years ago, the late Earl Nightingale, an American motivational speaker known as the Dean of Personal Development, electrified his sales team at his insurance company with a message—the "strangest secret"—that would eventually motivate millions of people worldwide. In essence, the strangest secret is, "You are what you think; you are your thoughts." For those of you who might be students of history and philosophy, you know that as powerful as this message is, it is not a new one. Abraham Lincoln said, "People are about as happy as they make up their minds to be." Ralph Waldo Emerson said, "We become what we think about all day long." William Shakespeare said, "There is nothing either good or bad, but thinking makes it so." And Jesus said, "As you think, so shall you be."

There are some employment authorities and job coaches who would tell you that during difficult economic times and during periods of high unemployment, the most important asset you have is not your savings account, your house, or even your skills and qualifications. They would argue that the most important asset you have is your job. No doubt, your job or source of income is a valuable asset; but I would argue that your most valuable asset is your thoughts—your ability to think and, more important, your ability to change how you think!

CHANGE YOUR THINKING; CHANGE YOUR LIFE

You are about to embark on a job transition campaign. Having said this, let me pose to you some questions to think about: are you planning on conducting your campaign with high energy, enthusiasm, and confidence? What are your beliefs about seeking out a new job or identifying a new career?

What are your beliefs about the economy and the current state of the job market? What are your beliefs about résumés and interviewing? What are your beliefs about how many hours you will invest in landing a new, more rewarding job? And what are your beliefs about how others will perceive you if you have been downsized or are unemployed?

You see, *most of your beliefs are merely your thoughts that have been conditioned or programmed into your mind.* For instance, when you experience a job loss, the automatic conditioned pattern of response is to think that this event is devastating, humiliating, and painful. You involuntarily associate fear with joblessness because that is how you've been conditioned to react. On the other hand, you can consciously and authentically change your beliefs about job loss and look at the event as a gift and as an opportunity to improve yourself, your income, and your future. The situation of losing a job is just that, a job loss. The emotions associated with this event, be they positive or negative, are derived from your beliefs—how you think—about losing a job. In other words, it's not the events in your life that make the difference between happiness and unhappiness. Rather, it's the meaning and beliefs that you associate with those events. It's how you think.

Sarah Hightower Hill, president and CEO of Chandler-Hill Partners, a national executive outplace firm based in Tucson, Arizona, says:

> *Who is doing your thinking? With the onslaught of 24-hour news and a challenging economy and job market being the primary topics of conversation by all of the talking heads and their analysts, it's difficult if not impossible to keep from being prejudiced in some way by what you hear. My point in asking "who is doing your thinking," is to call attention to what happens when you allow others to do your thinking and the negative impact it can have. Recently I had a conversation with an executive client who was seeking to reenter the job market quickly. I was surprised when he told me that he thought it best to wait six to nine months before beginning his campaign because there are no jobs out there at this time. This client had a master's degree, plenty of experience, and a professional designation. Yet, because the*

national news, family members, and friends convinced him that there were no jobs to be had, he was willing to put off his job search for six to nine months. What would be the cost of that mistake? If he had been earning $100k a year, the cost of waiting six months would cost him a minimum of $50k. What I am suggesting is that you always question who is doing your thinking because, many times, it's based on erroneous or misleading data and information.

In one of the first books ever published on career management, *Pick Your Job and Land It!,* published in 1938, authors Sidney and Mary Edlund made it clear that one's mental outlook (beliefs) determines outcome. In 1932, during the Great Depression, a good friend of the Edlunds lost his job and associated massive pain and a sense of despair with this event. The Edlunds helped their friend change the meaning of the event by helping him to change his beliefs. First, they pointed out that if he were to associate the idea of having fun with pursuing a new job, even with a 23.6 percent unemployment rate, he'd not only succeed in finding a new job quickly, but actually enjoy the process. The Edlunds also challenged their friend to change his beliefs about the job hunt itself. They suggested he look at it, not as a job hunt where he would be begging for jobs, but rather as a marketing and sales campaign where he offered valuable services that would benefit a company during difficult economic times.

In an economy where almost one in four people was out of work, this person was offered a job in less than a month because he changed his beliefs, his way of thinking. By changing his thinking, he changed his organizational strategies and methods of securing a new job. And to further drive home the fact that when you change your thinking, you can change any aspect of your life, the Edlunds noted that their friend actually beat out two close acquaintances and one family member of the hiring manager because he raised the bar of conducting an efficient high-impact campaign that he genuinely enjoyed.

YOU CONTROL HOW YOU THINK

People have the unique ability to change whenever they make the decision to do so. How you deal with adversity will shape your life more than almost anything else. If you associate pain, fear, and failure with job loss, you may begin to believe that there's nothing you can do to make things better. You'll risk developing a sense of hopelessness or outright depression. These beliefs are destructive beliefs, and the achievement of success becomes almost impossible. On the other hand, when you realize that your belief system is not healthy emotionally and is not supporting your goals, ambitions, and potential, you can change how you think instantly! Nothing has to change in order for you to feel better about something except the meaning you give to it based on the thoughts you attach to it.

Is the Glass Half Empty or Half Full?

One of the best examples of the power of a belief is that age-old question, is the glass half empty or half full? If you perceive the glass as half empty, you'll probably have an empty and painful experience. If you alter your belief and view the glass as half full, you'll have a much better chance of experiencing a feeling of optimism, hope, and pleasure. Same glass, same amount of liquid in the glass, but different emotions and feelings based on your beliefs—how you think!

No human being had ever run a mile in under four minutes. However, in 1954 Roger Banister did just that. But there's a greater story hidden behind this story. After Banister did what no human had ever accomplished, 37 other people broke the four-minute mile within a 12-month period. Can you begin to see how changing a belief can result in an almost miraculous achievement? Once Banister broke the four-minute-mile barrier, *he also broke the belief barrier* for others. As a result, runners instantly adopted a new belief that breaking the four-minute mile was achievable. Once you believe that you can overcome and successfully work through a job loss, or any life or career challenge for that matter, because others have successfully done so, you get a renewed sense of confidence and a strong feeling of certainty that you, too, can achieve the same successful results.

The bottom line here is that *you determine how you think at any given time based on how you manage and control your thoughts and beliefs.* And this is important, because many traditional job search beliefs will be challenged throughout this book, and you must be open to examining and changing your beliefs about the entire process of career and job transition.

What Are Your Beliefs about Landing a New Job?

Consider the following beliefs and the consequences, both positive and negative, that would result if you were to adopt one versus the other:

This is a bad economy, and there are no good jobs available.
This is a challenging economy, but there are plenty of well-paying jobs just waiting for me if I work smarter and harder than my competitors.

The job search is a painful and humiliating experience.
The job campaign will be enjoyable and a character-building endeavor.

It will take me forever to land a new job.
Armed with the right tools and strategies, I can land a new job quickly.

I'll never find another job that will pay me what I was earning before.
I know my value, the results I can produce, and the benefits I bring to a new employer. This will position me to land a better-paying job in no time.

My family and friends will look down at me because I don't have a job; this is embarrassing and humiliating.
With a confident attitude, my family and friends will support my job transition efforts and will be a positive influence in landing my next job.

My résumé must conform to traditional standards and blend in with all other résumés.

My résumé can be an exciting and informative marketing document that communicates my value and sets me apart from my competition.

Résumés are only beneficial for getting my foot in the door.

Résumés are important documents that identify value, instill a sense of confidence, and strengthen me as an interviewee so I can land a new, more rewarding job.

An interview is a forum where I am judged, and I don't like being judged.

An interview is just an encounter where two parties gather together to determine whether they can meet each other's needs in an amicable and friendly manner.

I don't need a written plan of action to get a job. I'll just wing it.

If I fail to develop a written strategic action plan, I can expect to fail; so I will develop the best written plan possible to achieve my job goals.

I hate networking. I'll never get a good job because I don't have a strong network of contacts.

I'll enjoy the process of establishing a *personal sales team*, made up of people I know and new relationships I will cultivate, who will assist me to land the perfect job.

I am too old to get a new job. There is definite age discrimination against older workers like me.

I will land a new job based on my ability to produce results, not on my age.

I can't afford to spend money on getting a new job because I have no job.

I can't afford *not* to invest in getting a new job even if I have no job, because if I don't invest in my future, I may not have one.

Beliefs Will Either Empower or Limit Success Achievement

No doubt you are well aware of the concept of the self-fulfilling prophecy. The definition of a self-fulfilling prophecy is that negative beliefs predict or manifest negative behavior. Interestingly enough, we don't associate the self-fulfilling prophecy with positive beliefs to manifest positive events. But in truth, your beliefs, whether they are positive or negative, empowering or limiting, will determine behavior and influence outcome. The concept of the self-fulfilling prophecy is normally associated with negative beliefs that result in limited achievement or downright disaster. The challenge here is that this idea goes against the law of attraction and the concept of positive affirmations. The fact of the matter is, *if you associate positive beliefs with deep emotion, you can predict and manifest positive events.*

SUMMARY

Chekhov said that "man is what he believes," and that is certainly true when you begin the process of orchestrating a job transition campaign or dealing with work-related stress and challenges. I ask that you simply become aware of what your beliefs are and then ask yourself, "Do they empower me, or do they limit me in my quest for a better job or career, a better quality of life?" And if your belief system doesn't empower you to the extent you feel it must, know that you only need to adopt and embrace new beliefs that will fuel future success and promote achievement and personal happiness.

Now it's time to embark on the five-step process that will catapult you from where you are to where you want to be. The five-step process includes:

1. *Learning how to ride the emotional roller-coaster:* how to manage fear and emotions when adversity affects your world.
2. *Defining your goal:* If you don't know where you're going, it's hard to get there.
3. *Using value-based résumés and self-marketing tools:* Average résumés won't attract outstanding jobs.
4. *Creating a Meticulous Action Plan (MAP):* Don't look east to watch a sunset.
5. *Taking action:* "As ye sow, so shall ye reap."

LEARNING HOW TO RIDE THE EMOTIONAL ROLLER-COASTER

HOW TO MANAGE FEAR AND EMOTIONS WHEN ADVERSITY AFFECTS YOUR WORLD

Arguably, two of the most painful occurrences in life are the loss of a loved one and the loss of a job. That being said and given your own situation, what emotions are you feeling at this moment? Are you stunned, terrified, infuriated? Are you experiencing high anxiety or even bouts of depression? Are you in a place called "I can't believe this is happening to me" or "this must be a bad dream"? These are just some of the emotions experienced by people whose lives are turned upside down when they lose their jobs and find themselves seeking new opportunities in troubled economies and highly competitive job markets.

Regardless of what you are facing, in most cases, worry takes over and emotions go uncontrollably berserk. Initial questions will pervade your thoughts: "Will I survive this?" "Why did this happen to me?" "What did I do to deserve this?" "Will I be able to endure the pain?" "How long will this last?" "Where will the money come from?" "Will I be able to keep my home?" "How will this affect my quality of life?" "Will I be a burden to my family?" *The worst-case scenario takes center stage in the theater of your mind, and fear plays the starring role.*

Landing a new job in a troubled economy begins when you constructively and proactively manage and control your fears and emotions. *Success is born from a fearless constitution.* There are two primary components for effectively managing job loss and securing a new job. The first is to assume personal responsibility and maintain a confident and positive attitude. The second is to use your peak performing state of mind to plan and execute a flawless job transition campaign. You must become an educated, determined, and optimistic campaigner to effectively recover from job loss and land a new job in a competitive job market. *The information contained in this chapter goes far beyond the idea of positive thinking.* You will be introduced to specific techniques and strategies to inspire you to remain positive and to manage your fears and emotions no matter what challenges you face. By doing so, you become an empowered, proactive participant in securing a new opportunity quickly and effectively.

FIRST, A FEW WORDS ABOUT FEAR

Fear is normal—it can't be eliminated, nor should it be ignored. *Fear must be conquered.* It's been shown that experiencing success and landing a new, more rewarding job begins as soon as you learn how to conquer your fear. In fact, if you don't acknowledge your fear, you'll become more at risk psychologically. Disarming and conquering your fear begins with recognizing its presence, accepting it, and taking action to manage it. And fear grips not just those who have lost their jobs, but all those who are part of their circle of influence—spouses, children, parents, and friends.

This chapter contains authoritative information and strategies to motivate and empower everyone involved in the job transition process to effectively deal with fear and its attendant crippling emotions such as guilt, resentment, helplessness, and feelings of being overwhelmed. In the wake of some of life's most difficult moments, courage and confidence become the conquering heroes. Courage and confidence help you become courageous in the wake of fear, negativity, pessimism, and stress in your efforts to get a new job in troubled economies.

John Costello was a sales professional working in his family's business. He was unable to meet his financial obligations for himself and his son, Francesco, and he sought a new job. He said: "My emotions were on a constant roller-coaster ride. One day I was hopeful that my contacts would help me find a new position. Then anger, fear, and despair took over. I realized I was going to need help working through my emotions. And when I learned how to take control of my emotions, I immediately took control of my future in a positive and successful manner. I landed the job I wanted in less than two months."

A positive attitude and confident approach to job loss not only makes the associated traumas and dramas bearable, but will also result in securing a new job quickly and enjoyably. International job coach Martin Buckland, JCTC and principal of Elite Executive Career Management Services headquartered in Ontario, Canada, says, "Controlling negative emotions in a positive way is critical to any job search campaign. The more out of control you are, the longer the campaign will take, and you probably won't land the kind of job you really deserve. I work as hard with clients on their emotions as I do on their résumés."

So as you begin your journey to secure a new opportunity, you must embrace two critical components:

1. Adopt a healthy and positive outlook about how best to cope with and work through your job loss, as well as any of life's other unexpected bumps in the road.
2. Master the 10 principles of success and the four emotional channeling techniques I will introduce later in this chapter to help you maintain a positive, healthy state of mind.

YOUR QUALITY OF LIFE *IS* THE QUALITY OF YOUR EMOTIONS

Your quality of life—and that includes how you feel—is the quality of your emotions. It's not what you drive, where you live, or what you're experiencing that matters; it's how you feel about what you drive, where you live, or what you're experiencing that makes all the difference. Managing your emotions and moods is about not allowing anyone or anything to determine how you feel regardless of the challenges you face. You have the ultimate power to determine how you feel at any given time and in any situation.

There are so many variables that influence how you feel. The irony is that if you're like most people, you allow everything and everyone, except you, to determine what you are feeling. Said differently, *you allow external influences to dictate your emotions.* Advertisers, television programs, and the media are external influences. Parents, family members, and friends are external influences. Teachers, professors, and spiritual leaders are external influences. Even employment professionals—including job coaches, authors, HR managers, and executive recruiters—are external influences. Most of the time, you allow other people and other people's expectations to dictate how you feel. But seldom do you allow yourself to determine how you feel based on your own conscious thoughts and expectations of yourself. Your reactions and emotions are a result of subconscious or conditioned beliefs rather than reason and common sense. In others words, you simply react in a fear-based, negative manner to situations, rather than rationally and constructively address and manage them.

Destructive, negative, or fear-based emotions are emotions that hurt you and others. They are emotions that damage the job transition process and impede prospects of landing a job! Nothing good can come from something bad if negativity and fear drive the emotional process.

If you face your adversities in a courageous and positive manner, you can make the best of any circumstance. *The bottom line is that you have the power to control how you feel at any moment, no matter what the situation.* As an example, two women experience the ultimate pain, the death of a child by a drunk driver. Both women experience unbearable grief. One woman commits suicide and destroys her life and the lives of those she leaves behind. The other, Candy Lightner, forms MADD (Mothers Against Drunk Driving). What was the difference? The difference was mindset!

"HOW"—THE MISSING LINK

Like a world-class athlete, mindset determines outcome; emotions determine success, or a lack thereof. *You can have superior skills, but if you don't show up to play emotionally, you'll lose!* In most cases, underdogs win not by having superior skills, but by having a bigger heart, a stronger character, and a positive, unstoppable mindset. So when job loss and career issues create situations and events that require you to be at your emotional best, how do you do it? In other words, when well-meaning people tell you to "think positive" in the midst of crisis and chaos, how do you do this? Or better yet, how do you alter your emotions so that you actually benefit from the predicament you face? You're challenged to take the "high road" when you lose a job. You're advised to turn adversity into opportunity and to make the best of a bad situation. But once again, the question is, how do you accomplish this? The material in this chapter will teach you how. But before we delve into the how, you must know "The Five Musts" for changing your state of mind to quickly and successfully land the job you want at the pay you deserve in a troubled economy with high unemployment.

1. *You must want to change.* You must make the decision to change and have a deep-rooted desire to be in total command of your emotional state at all times.
2. *You must be committed to change.* Commitment means you'll pay any price to attain your goals. Commitment means that quitting is not an option and that you'll be relentless in pursuit of your objectives.
3. *You must employ massive discipline in order to change.* Discipline means doing what you don't want to do in pursuit of what you want to achieve. Discipline means being aware of how you feel—and knowing

your emotions are *not* productive. Discipline means mastering just a few of the techniques that will be introduced in this chapter so you remain cool and calm and in emotional control to achieve your job goals.

4. *You must embrace discomfort to ensure change.* Here's one of the more profound statements I'll make in this chapter: *discomfort cures "dis-ease."* Physical therapy might be uncomfortable, but it will cure the dis-ease of a possible relapse or prolonged recovery. And networking and investing more time and energy in attaining a new job might be discomforting at first, but it will cure the dis-ease of continued unemployment. Discomfort is a gift. It's complacency and procrastination that induce poverty of the mind and atrophy of the spirit and rob you of any chance of landing a job, especially in a troubled economy. Complacency impairs any chance of success, whereas discomfort opens many new doors of opportunity.

5. *You must condition yourself to learn new techniques to achieve lasting change.* Once you've learned the disciplines of managing your emotions and approach your job and career challenges with a fearless constitution, you must condition yourself to master the techniques so they become second nature. Consistent repetition of new concepts and ideas is a success strategy. If you start to walk an hour a day to improve your health and increase your energy so you can work harder and smarter at landing a new job, you must condition this activity so it becomes routine. If you send out 15 résumés, contact five people in your network, and spend three hours online every day to secure a new job, this activity must become habitual so you give yourself a clear advantage over other qualified candidates in securing the best opportunities that await you.

THE 10 PRINCIPLES FOR SUCCESS

Before I introduce you to four powerful emotional channeling techniques, techniques that will enable you to remain upbeat, positive, and optimistic during difficult times, I want to first teach you the 10 principles for successfully obtaining a new job in troubled economies. These principles are not new; in fact they're old. I believe that the list of 10 principles that I have assembled represents the critical philosophies and strategies for winning a new job. Once you have a clear understanding of these 10 principles and embrace them, the emotional channeling techniques presented later in this chapter will work more effectively and at lightning speed to produce a courageous constitution that will result in a new and rewarding job!

And I need to point out here that you can't simply pick and choose which of the 10 principles you like and which you'd like to ignore. *All 10 must be mastered with equal passion.* Landing a job in a competitive job market requires that you become proficient with all 10 principles.

Principle #1: Personal Responsibility: *If It's Going to Be, It's Up to Me*

The two major causes of underachievement are blame and excuses. Sadly, few people seem willing to take personal responsibility these days. Taking responsibility means accepting any type of wind that might blow, knowing that it's not the wind, but rather the set of the sail that makes the difference between unemployment and gainful employment, between remaining in a stressful job and securing the perfect job. Taking responsibility means that *if it's going to be, it's up to me and no one else!* Responsibility means going the extra mile with a smile, knowing that *going the extra mile is the best investment you can make in yourself and your future.* Taking personal responsibility means *not* taking the path of least resistance even though it's a seductive option, but paying any price needed to succeed.

Responsibility means being a proactive and supportive resource in your own job transition campaign. You have a choice. You can spend 95 percent of your time and energy on the problem, blaming, finding excuses, and griping that the world is unfair. Or you can take personal responsibility and invest 95 percent of your time and energy on the solution, pursuing your career objectives with passion and confidence, knowing only you can stand in the way of your own success.

Principle #2: Desire: *Nothing Happens without First a Dream*

Purpose is everything. Being "on purpose" means you're willing to commit to your dreams, desires, job, and career goals. Commitment means that you'll never give up on your quest for a better life, no matter what obstacles stand in your way, because you're driven to succeed. As long as the flame of desire burns deep within you, you'll achieve whatever it is you want to achieve, because *all new job opportunities are born from a burning desire.* A burning desire creates inner drive, and when you're driven to land a new and exciting job, all sorts of opportunities will present themselves. It's true that *whatever your mind can conceive and believe, you can achieve.* Believe in yourself and your goals. When the purpose is clear and when you're driven to pursue and secure a better job, you will.

Principle #3: Faith: *Where There's a Will, There's a Way*

Faith is that ethereal power of knowing that miracles are born from obscurity when you believe. Faith is a belief, or a feeling of certainty, that something good can be created even though it has yet to be determined when or how it will occur. The expression "I'll believe it when I see it" is actually not the success formula for landing a new position. The formula that will help you get a job in a troubled job market is the opposite: "I'll see it when I first believe it." You first have to believe you can secure your next job; then you will.

Faith can be the belief that a higher power will help be a catalyst for the manifestation of your career goals. Or faith can be the unconditional belief that you have the power to achieve your mission. *In any case, faith is that intangible, positive energy needed to land a job in a troubled job market. The how hasn't arrived in your mind yet, but you have faith that it will.* Faith means that you are certain that you will secure a new job because you know that anything is possible if you truly believe it is.

Principle #4: A "Healthy" Character: *Success Achievement Is Not Attracted by an Unhealthy Constitution*

A healthy character means developing a positive outlook on life no matter what serious situation you're facing. Well-respected basketball coach John Wooden said, "Be more concerned about your character than your reputation. Your reputation is how others perceive you; your character is who you really are." Character means having a healthy, positive attitude in the wake of job loss or any life challenge. Clement Stone said, "There is little difference in people, but that little difference makes a big difference. The little difference is attitude. The big difference is whether it is positive or negative." Thomas Jefferson said, "Nothing can stop a person with the right mental attitude from achieving his goal; but nothing on earth can help the person with the wrong mental attitude."

A healthy character means having the ability to use the right, honest, constructive thought, action, or reaction with any person, situation, or set of circumstances. It allows you to build on hope to overcome the feeling of despair and discouragement. A healthy character gives you the mental power, a feeling of confidence and positive expectation, to achieve anything at any time no matter what obstacles you face. Anyone can maintain a good attitude when things are going well. It's when the going gets tough that a healthy character inspires the tough to get going. *One of the best methods for developing a healthy character is to appreciate all that you presently have.* Most people tend to focus on what they don't have rather than on the many gifts they actually possess. A healthy character comes from a sincere appreciation for all that you have today in pursuit of all that you want tomorrow.

Principle #5: Discipline: *Without Discipline, Nothing Is Possible*

Discipline is the bridge between employment and unemployment, between underemployment and meaningful employment. *Discipline means doing those things that others aren't willing to do and hanging in there long after everyone else has let go.* Discipline is the foundation upon which all success is attained. An abundance of discipline leads to an abundance of job offers! In reality, you have one of two life-changing choices to make: to employ discipline today to achieve your job objectives or neglect to employ discipline at the expense of your goals.

Discipline leads to reward. Neglect leads to regret. The great Vince Lombardi said, "Discipline and mental toughness are many things and rather difficult to explain. Its qualities are sacrifice and self-denial, and most importantly, it's combined with a perfectly disciplined will that refuses to give in."

The key is to choose discipline over "easy." You don't get to the World Series or the Olympics by easy, and you don't become a successful sales professional, nurse, administrative assistant, or CEO by easy. There is no "easy button" for landing a job in a troubled economy with high rates of unemployment. You get there through discipline.

Principle #6: A Positive Sphere of Influence: *Your Environment May Determine How Quickly You'll Land Your Next Job!*

Will Rogers may have said it best when he said that "the quality of life is often a result of the people in life you avoid." It's important to consistently assess the people you spend time with and determine if they are with you or against you in identifying, pursuing, and getting a new job or career. A president of a corporation is affected by those people serving on the board of directors. The president of the United States is affected by advisers and those in the cabinet. World-class athletes and entertainers surround themselves with world-class coaches and advisers. *You, too, must have a positive, high-energy, and world-class group of advisers to help you meet your job and career objectives.* This sphere of influence can be made up of a support group, job coaches, therapists, family members, and friends. The primary criterion for membership in your sphere of influence is that all members must be supportive of you and your goals. No, they don't always have to agree with you.

You want constructive debate! But when they don't agree, they must do so in a compassionate and tactful manner.

Remember, influence can be subtle, so you must always be aware and evaluate those people you spend time with on a regular basis. Once aware of your sphere of influence, you'll want to determine whom you need to spend more time with, whom you need to spend less time with, whom you need to meet and add to your sphere of influence, and whom you need to disassociate with, either partially or completely. Demand more of yourself and of those you spend time with. When the demands are high, you'll achieve a new job or a more lucrative opportunity swiftly and enjoy the process along the way.

Principle #7: Embrace Adversity and Struggle: *Strengthen Your Achievement Muscles*

Who ever came up with the expression, "Get it right the first time?" Who ever gets it right the first time? In fact, we're not supposed to get it right the first time. Thomas Edison failed nearly 10,000 times trying to invent the lightbulb. Walt Disney was turned down hundreds of times in his attempts to finance Disneyland. Babe Ruth struck out twice as many times as he hit home runs. Babies don't walk the first time they try. You probably don't want to read this, but *adversity is the catalyst for all success. Massive failure leads to massive success.* It's exciting to know that in every adversity lies the seed of a major opportunity. Did you learn how to read the first time you were introduced to the alphabet? No, you struggled with it. Yet because of the struggle, you can read this book!

Can you begin to see that failure is a human-made illusion of a perfectly natural phenomenon? In actuality, there is no such thing as failure; struggle yes, failure no! The human experience requires that you struggle for anything meaningful in life because it's the only way you can appreciate anything. How can there be meaning to life without an appreciation for life? We've created a monster by creating the concept of failure. *Failure doesn't exist except when the fear of trying inhibits or outright prevents any attempt to achieve your potential.*

The following story best illustrates the natural phenomenon of struggle and why struggle is a critical component and necessary ingredient for landing a job in tough times.

The Butterfly Story

The wise old man of the village held a cocoon in the palm of his hand.

"What's that?" the young boy asked.

"Why it's a cocoon," replied the wise man. "Inside is a caterpillar that spun this cocoon. And when he's ready, he'll turn into a wondrous butterfly and break out of the cocoon."

"Oh, can I have it?" asked the young boy.

"Of course," answered the wise man. "But first you must promise that you won't open the cocoon for the butterfly when he begins to break out. The butterfly must do it all by himself. Can you promise me that?"

The young boy agreed and took the cocoon home with him.

The next day, the cocoon began to tremble, and the butterfly fought hard to escape it. The young boy couldn't bear to watch the butterfly struggle, and after a short while, he broke open the cocoon to help the butterfly escape. The beautiful butterfly soared into the air and suddenly, and quite unexpectedly, plummeted to the ground ... and died.

The boy returned to the village wise man, crying and cradling the dead butterfly in his hand.

"Did you help the butterfly escape from the cocoon?" the wise man asked.

"Yes," replied the child.

"What you didn't understand," the wise man said, "was that the butterfly had to struggle in order to build strength in his wings. By working hard to get out, the butterfly was building muscles that he needed in order to fly. By trying to make it easier for him, you actually

made it harder for him, in this case, impossible, to fly. You killed him with good intentions."

So when you experience a so-called failure, don't view this as failure, but rather as a "character muscle-building" process. It's a process that will strengthen your resolve to transform your career much the same way a caterpillar transforms itself into an elegant butterfly. The job campaign necessitates that you embrace struggle and constructively address adversity. When you do so, new opportunities will present themselves sooner than you'd think possible.

Principle #8: Fitness and Energy: *Be Kind to Your Body; It's the Only One You Have*

You are dealing with a high-stress challenge: *getting a new job in a troubled economy requires massive amounts of energy.* Both physical and emotional well-being are important to assure future success. Two strategies for intensifying your energy level and overall well-being are 1) proper nutrition and 2) consistent exercise. You must commit to developing a health plan now and for the rest of your life. It can be as simple as taking a walk around the block, eating an apple a day, and reducing the intake of any substances that impede fitness and energy.

This is not the forum to provide an extensive set of guidelines for improving your health and energy. But there are eight basic tips that will jump-start the process. These simple health and fitness tips are regimens that will give you the enthusiastic energy to land your next job.

1. Walk briskly as often as you can, every day if possible.
2. Reduce your portions; don't overeat. When you're full, stop eating!
3. Drink more water and eliminate soda.
4. Find time every day to meditate, relax, and think positive thoughts. You will then be able to come up with new ideas to meet your goals.
5. Eat more vegetables, fruit, soy products, and organic foods.
6. Reduce your intake of dairy products and red meat.

7. Reduce your intake of caffeine, alcohol, illegal drugs, and tobacco.

8. Whenever you get the chance to move, move! Climb the stairs rather than take the elevator. Don't drive when you can walk. Don't look for the closest parking spot. And if you are restricted health-wise, work with your medical team to see what steps you can take to indulge in some form of exercise to improve your energy and fitness.

Do your best to increase your energy level and recruit fitness as a key component to your job transition strategy. And this begins with the development of a healthy nutrition and exercise plan.

Principle #9: Acknowledge and Master Your Fears: *Courage Is the Antidote to Fear*

As I've said from the get-go, fear is the main impediment to success. The primary obstacle that stands in the way of getting your next job is fear. Fear is debilitating and incapacitating. That said, courage is the antidote to fear. *Courage*, according to Mark Twain, is *"resistance to fear, mastery over fear, but not an absence of fear."* That's what makes heroes—courage, in the face of, not the absence of, fear. And that's what facilitates a successful and satisfying job campaign.

At this point, it's important that I acknowledge that the fear of losing a loved one as well as losing a job is real, and it won't go away. Emotional and physical pain, stress, and downright terror are permanent supporting cast members on the stage of life. *The goal is not to try and eliminate them, because they won't leave the stage! The objective, however, is to learn how to neutralize and effectively manage them.* Landing your next job begins with the understanding that fear is ever present, but will never be allowed to play a starring role. The all-important topic of learning and mastering fear management techniques is covered next in this chapter when you learn the power of emotional channeling. But before we address four emotional channeling techniques, let's conclude with the tenth principle; the one often referred to as the *miracle principle.*

Principle #10: Take Action: *The Miracle Principle*

All the planning in the world, all the processes, models, and strategies for landing a job in a troubled job market, means absolutely nothing unless fueled by action. It is sometimes said that the road to Hell is paved with good intentions, but the road to your next job is paved with activity and positive action. Action, driven by discipline, is what propels the process leading to an effective job campaign. It's often been said that most people know what to do but don't do what they know. We've all heard the expression, "Actions speak louder than words." *When you take massive action, you'll get massive results.*

Years ago, a teacher advised me to *make rest a necessity, not an objective.* Yes, you need to rest in order to revitalize and regain the energy required to take more action to achieve your goals. Common sense would dictate that even if you follow the first nine principles to a tee, without taking massive action, securing a new job is near impossible. It's action that will result in you landing your next opportunity in difficult job markets.

SUMMARY

You now know the 10 philosophical principles that will help you identify, pursue, and secure the job you want at the pay you deserve. Embrace these 10 principles, and you'll achieve a level of success and inner calm you never dreamed possible. Is this easy? You bet it is! All you have to do is work diligently at what's easy. When you commit to these 10 principles, you'll be working at your next job before you know it!

EMOTIONAL CHANNELING TECHNIQUES: FOUR TECHNIQUES FOR MANAGING FEAR AND EMOTIONS DURING JOB LOSS

Emotional channeling techniques are specific strategies practiced by world-class athletes, entertainers, and business and political leaders to deal with and overcome adversity, setbacks, and obstacles. These techniques teach you how to think positively during negative and difficult times. They'll help you remain calm and emotionally balanced when you are in the midst of job loss and when you face frustration during the job transition campaign. *Emotional channeling is personalized success conditioning.* It's the process of using specific techniques to consciously and proactively manage your state of mind on a continual basis to positively react to, and overcome, job loss or any other career or life setback.

Awareness and Desire: The Keys to Successful Channeling

Emotional channeling requires both keen awareness and a burning desire: the awareness that you're in, or entering, a negative or fear-based emotional state and the desire to want to alter that state. If someone says something offensive to you, you must be aware that you're losing your cool and have a desire to control your anger. *Emotional channeling is only effective when you are aware that something is triggering a negative or fear-based emotional state. Once aware that you're on the verge of losing emotional control, you must have a desire to neutralize or outright eliminate that negative or fear-based emotion.* If you continually raise your level of awareness, you'll continually improve your skills to properly manage your emotions and your temper. When this happens, you'll be in a better state of mind to conduct a flawless job transition campaign and get that special job.

Below are four techniques that are highly effective when facing job loss and difficult career or life issues. Mind you, they won't make your problems go away! They will, however, allow you to get into a more empowered and positive mindset so you can quickly and, believe it or not, more enjoyably resolve them.

Emotional Channeling Technique #1: Ask Courageous Questions

How do I raise the bar of dealing with my job loss and, as well, set an example for my family and friends, so if they ever have to face a similar crisis, they'll do so with class and dignity? The Socratic method is a form of thoughtful inquiry where you explore the implications of your beliefs and those of others by asking high-quality questions to stimulate new thoughts and resolve issues and challenges. The powerful art of asking *higher-quality questions* is considered the oldest and most effective teaching strategy for fostering critical thinking and resolving job loss and job-related problems. Indeed, the quality of the questions you ask yourself and others determines the quality of answers you receive. The quality of answers you receive, in turn, determines the quality of emotions you experience and, thus, the speed in which you'll land a new job.

Socrates understood that the human brain is programmed to answer any question it's asked. For instance, if you ask the question, "Why me, God?" in the midst of a job loss, you might respond with, "I must have done something wrong to deserve this," or "I must not be very lucky and am just doomed to struggle my entire life." If you ask the question, "How will I ever make the same amount of money in my next job given this hideous economy?" you'll probably answer with, "I must simply accept the reality that I'll never make what I'm worth again." These types of questions are called *destructive questions* because they result in further emotional conflict and anguish. Destructive questions seldom resolve anything in a constructive and positive manner.

If, on the other hand, you ask the question, "What lessons can I learn by losing my job?" you might respond with, "I'm learning courage and patience, and I'm setting the stage for a better job, better pay, and a better quality of life." If you ask the question, "Even though this is a difficult economy, what must I do to ensure that I make as much money as I made before?" you might answer with, "I must identify my value and make sure I communicate my value in a powerful résumé and throughout my entire job campaign. No doubt, if I am able to communicate my value, I'll earn even more than I did at my last job." These are called *courageous questions*. Courageous questions always lead to courageous answers that will inspire you to take the appropriate action to land a new job, no matter how challenging the economy or job market is. Courageous questions, if asked with high emotion, always result in high-quality, life-enhancing answers.

Tom Dempsey is widely known for his NFL record 63-yard field goal that he kicked in the final two seconds of a game to give his team, the New Orleans Saints, a 19–17 win over the Detroit Lions on November 8, 1970. But the real story is that Dempsey was born with half a right foot and no right hand. He had an unquenchable desire to be a professional football player, and as a result, his parents asked courageous and high-quality questions. Rather than ask, "How can you possibly play football in your condition?" Dempsey's parents asked a better question, "What can be done so Tom can pursue his dream?" As a result of asking a courageous question, an artificial foot and a modified shoe were made for him. Tom Dempsey's dream came true, and he became a professional football player.

EXAMPLES OF COURAGEOUS QUESTIONS

Courageous questions are questions that inspire answers to quell or significantly reduce fear, negativity, and a bad temper, to ignite the flame of hope and promote a successful job campaign. Consider the following:

Destructive question: Why does this always happen to me?
Courageous question: How can I use this to my advantage?

Destructive question: Why can't things be easier?
Courageous question: How can I become tougher and wiser?

Destructive question: When will things turn around for me?
Courageous question: How can I enjoy turning things around myself?

Destructive question: Will my spouse support me through this ordeal?
Courageous question   How can we grow closer going through this?

Destructive question: Will I ever get a new job at the same pay?
Courageous question: What do I have to learn and whom do I have to meet to ensure I get a better job at a higher rate of pay?

Destructive question: How long will this job search last?
Courageous question: What action must I take to land a job quickly?

Destructive question: What kind of burden will I be to my family?

Courageous question: How can I be an example to my family and make the best of a difficult situation?

Destructive question: How will I ever get through this?

Courageous question   How have I successfully dealt with challenges in the past?

Below are just a few of the infinite questions that, if asked with high emotion and a deep desire to seek out constructive answers, will stimulate new thoughts to resolve your job and career challenges. By asking courageous questions, your brain will come up with seemingly miraculous answers so that you'll better manage negativity and fear. And when you better manage negativity and fear, you'll be in a much better state of mind to pursue and land your next job.

- How have others effectively dealt with this problem in the past?
- How do I turn this problem into an adventure and meet this challenge with a positive outlook?
- What can I learn from this, and how can I enjoy the process?
- What resources are available to me in the community that will assist me in getting a new job?
- What do I need to research to gain better control of my future?
- Whom can I recruit for my job transition campaign "board of directors" that will advise me and support my efforts in a positive way?
- How can I be a hero to myself and others by meeting this challenge head-on with confidence and self-respect?
- Am I spending more time on the solution than on the problem?
- Am I displaying leadership qualities to the members of my family so they can be proud of me?
- What do I have to read to make myself a more educated job campaigner?

- How can I make those I love more comfortable and at ease with my situation?
- Whom do I have to meet so I can achieve my goals quickly?

When you begin to ask courageous questions, you'll challenge yourself to come up with life-changing, job-producing answers. When the right courageous questions are asked on a consistent basis, you'll come up with inspiring answers that will open doors to your next job opportunity.

Emotional Channeling Technique #2: Focus Management

This technique is one of the most effective channeling techniques to induce constructive emotional shifts for identifying, pursuing, and landing your next job. The primary concept behind focus management is to get you to voluntarily change your focus when you're in the midst of an emotional crisis or challenge. This technique works wonders simply by shifting your attention away from what's troubling you and focusing instead on something that's calming and comforting.

FOCUS IS ABOUT ATTENTION—WHAT YOU PAY ATTENTION TO

Human beings are strange creatures when it comes to what they focus on. Isn't it true that 10 great things can happen to you today along with just 1 bad thing, and in most cases, you'll go home and burden your family and yourself with that 1 bad thing while never even acknowledging the 10 good things? I know I've done that. So why is it that most people tend not to focus on the positive and fully engage themselves on the negative? The answer is simple. That's the way they were conditioned.

What's most exciting about this channeling technique is that you can easily recondition yourself to focus (or refocus) on those things that will help you reduce stress, overcome fear, and control your temper. You can live a high-quality life even if you are out of a job and struggling to pay the bills simply by paying attention to what you're paying attention to. By doing this, you can then refocus your thoughts on more positive aspects of your life to help you through the tough times. In other words, you can change your focus!

FOCUS IS POWER

If you watch television and find that the constant bad news gets you down, you can continue focusing on the bad news and become more distraught, or you can shift your focus and change the station to one that is showing a comedy. You can go from a state of anguish to uncontrollable laughter—instantly!

The key to focus management is to first be aware of all the gifts you have currently in your life. When you lose a job, don't win an interview, or face rejection after rejection during the job transition campaign, you have the power to focus on things that are going well in your life, things you have to be thankful for. When life isn't going the way you'd like and your emotions start to come unglued, you have the ability to refocus on the positive aspects of your life to offset those negative emotions. *Are you focusing on the 10 percent unemployment rate or the 90 percent employment rate? Wouldn't you give anything for a 90 percent chance of winning the lottery?* Most countries of the world would give anything for a 90 percent employment rate. You see, when you refocus on the things that you are grateful for, the result will be happiness, hope, and peace of mind. With these new inspiring emotions, you'll set the stage to get the job you want in any kind of economy.

Joe DiMaggio had a father who consistently called him "good for nothing" throughout his youth. Why? Joe couldn't work in the family fish business because he got sick from the smell of fish. This didn't sit well with Joe's father, who thought Joe was just plain lazy. Even though his father's criticism created immeasurable pain, Joe refocused his attention, not on his father's anger and disappointment, but on his love of baseball. By redirecting his focus, Joe DiMaggio was able to manage his emotions and become one of the greatest players to ever play professional baseball. And his father was his greatest fan!

So here's a question for you. Whom do you love most in the world? The next time you get into an emotional quagmire where you're focusing on something that upsets you, know that you have the power to instantly refocus your attention away from that negative emotion and onto the people you love. What do you have to be grateful for? The next time you begin a typical temper tantrum, know that you have the power to instantly refocus your attention away from whatever set you off onto all that you have to be grateful for. It's that easy, just like switching from one television station to another!

In the October 2007 edition of *O, The Oprah Magazine*, the headline on the cover read "How to Calm Down, Cheer Up; Oprah's Guide to Soothing Your Mind." Oprah suggests that during difficult times, "Distract yourself. Put on music and dance; scrub the bathtub spotless, whatever engrosses you." *In other words, what Oprah is saying is, shift your focus!*

The essence of this emotional challenging technique is that you become acutely aware of what you're focusing on at all times. When you sense you're going into "overwhelm" or a fear-based emotional state, simply change your focus. The following is a short list of things you can focus on:

- The love of your family
- What you see
- What you smell
- What you feel
- What you hear
- What you taste
- Poetry
- Your pet
- Family photo albums
- Friendships

- Music
- Future dreams
- Happy memories
- A good movie
- A painting in your home
- Hobbies and interests
- Volunteer work
- Your good health
- A good book
- You live in the land of opportunity

Emotional Channeling Technique #3: Reference Validation

Reference validation is a technique where you *compare your situation to that of others who have successfully dealt with and overcome what you are currently experiencing. By doing so, you find strength and hope and learn specific strategies and concepts used by others so you too can effectively work through and resolve the issues you have.* Reference validation is a technique that instills a feeling of certainty and a feeling of confidence because someone else or a group of people have successfully overcome similar adversities and challenges that you now face.

A support group is a good example of reference validation. People in a support group share their experiences with one another. They gain strength and hope by validating that they too can effectively deal with the challenge at hand. The Workforce System has established One-Stops and offices throughout the country where former out-of-work employees address groups of current out-of-work employees. The former out-of-work employees share their experiences and strategies that led to new jobs. Possibly you have the loving support of your family and friends while you work through your job loss, but still they don't seem quite able to understand how you really feel or don't have the answers you are seeking. By attending sessions at a One-Stop or any job support group across the nation, the shared experiences of others will serve to give you hope and the confidence needed to resume your fighting spirit so you can secure a new employment opportunity.

A Little League baseball coach noticed that many of his players got angry and threw their bats in disgust after striking out. The coach sat the players down and told them that Babe Ruth hit over 700 home runs. He also pointed out that Babe Ruth struck out over 1,300 times! The coach explained that Babe Ruth didn't throw his bat. He just returned to the dugout to think about what he had to do differently the next time in order to hit a home run. He told the boys that it took 2 strikeouts for Babe Ruth to hit 1 home run. From that moment on, whenever a player struck out, he calmly walked back to the dugout to think about what he had to do the next time in order to get a hit. The coach was able to help change the negative emotional state and subsequent behavior (bat throwing and temper tantrums) by providing an example the boys could relate to. They had a new positive frame of reference to better deal with their unsuccessful attempts.

A life coach worked with Jason, a 15-year-old boy whose father violently and unexpectedly committed suicide. His mother asked the coach to help because Jason, a high school varsity basketball player, stated that all his dreams had died when his father died. The coach told Jason that dreams were meant to come true and that people can achieve their dreams if they are committed to them, regardless of circumstances and tragic events. The coach shared with Jason a story about a kid named Larry, a basketball player who wanted to become a professional. But like Jason, something happened to Larry that could have made this lifetime dream impossible. Larry's father also committed suicide. The coach had Jason's attention. He explained to Jason that Larry had come to a crossroad in his life and had two choices. He could give up on his dream of becoming a professional basketball player, or he could work hard to make the pros and dedicate his success to his father. Larry decided on the latter, and just a few years later, Larry Bird signed the largest rookie contract in the history of the NBA and became one of the game's greatest players. The coach gave Jason a new reference he could relate to. Once Jason understood that someone else had overcome a similar tragedy, this provided him with something that had been missing since his father's death—hope! Jason now had a new, powerful frame of reference to use to pursue his dreams.

Reference validation requires that you become a student of biographies, events, history, and even your own personal situations and those of your family members and friends. When you become aware of a negative or fear-based emotional shift, or experience a situation that begins to overwhelm you, you can immediately reference someone else who met and overcame a similar problem so you too can do the same.

To drive the point home, here's one more story. And, as a matter of fact, this person's story is legendary. He wanted a job, and that job was to become president of the United States. His business failed in 1831. He was defeated in his run for the Illinois State Legislature in 1832. His second business failed in 1833. He suffered a nervous breakdown in 1836. He was defeated in his run for Illinois House Speaker in 1838, and for his run for Congress in 1843. He was elected to Congress in 1846, but lost renomination in 1848. He lost his bid to the U.S. Senate in 1854, for vice president in 1856, and again for the U.S. Senate in 1858. Finally, in 1860, Abraham Lincoln was elected president of the United States.

When frustration and emotional anguish test your will when you lose a job and are struggling to win a new one in a tough economy, seek out references to cling to, much like a life vest. Maybe you, a friend, or a family member has gone through job loss before, so you can find references close to home on how best to get "back on the horse." You see, oftentimes you don't need to look far to find references to help guide you in a productive manner.

Emotional Channeling Technique #4: Humor Integration

We even have an expression for it; *laughter is the best medicine.* Faye was unexpectedly let go from her job. She was devastated and fearful. But she never lost her sense of humor. When asked what her occupation was a week after her termination, she responded that she was a *job search engineer.*

Humor can change the way you feel in an instant, if you seek it out. Many times, in the midst of fear or anguish, someone says a funny one-liner, and it breaks the ice for everyone else. *Just by asking the question, "What's funny about this?" you can change your emotions and how you feel, instantly.* My favorite character on *Saturday Night Live* was loudmouthed Roseanne Roseannadana played by Gilda Radner. Everything about Gilda Radner, from her quick wit to her wide grin, just cracked me up. To this day, she is, and will always be, my favorite comedian. So, like millions of others, I was truly saddened when I learned that Gilda was diagnosed with ovarian cancer back in 1986. Remember, now, that the loss of a loved one (or good friend) and the loss of a job result in very similar emotions, so cancer affects our physical and emotional well-being in the same way that joblessness does. Back to Gilda. Being a comedian, she used humor to deal with her own runaway fears and negativity. She used a unique and creative method of humor integration by writing a book entitled *It's Always Something.* The book was a story about her life and her battle with cancer. She wrote:

> *I started out to write a book called* A Portrait of the Artist as a Housewife. *I wanted to write a collection of stories and poems about things like my toaster oven and my relationships with plumbers, mailmen, and delivery people. But life dealt me a much more complicated story. Cancer is probably the most unfunny thing in the world, but I'm a comedian and even cancer couldn't stop me from seeing the*

humor in what I went through. So I'm sharing with you what I call a seriously funny book; one that confirms my father's favorite expression about life ... It's Always Something.

In a seriously funny way, Gilda analyzed and evaluated her disease, torment, and fear. There were passages in the book where she was full of hope when she received good news about her remission. She went into comical detail about certain procedures she had to endure and about how she reacted when she lost her hair from chemotherapy. By using humor in her writing, Gilda managed to put a positive spin on a very bad situation.

Gilda Radner wrote her book with the reasonable expectation that she could control the ending. She could not. She died in May 1989 at the age of 42. Gilda was fearless in her quest to deal with and overcome cancer, and she used humor to make the most out of every day she lived.

As you face your battle with joblessness and career issues, know that a dose of humor will go a long way in helping you achieve your career-related goals and objectives. Being out of a job temporarily is not a terminal disease. It's 100 percent curable! And I've discovered that a few chuckles along the road to your next job will go a long way in helping you get there sooner rather than later. Shared laughter is a significant emotional channeling technique that says, "I am not defeated; I have a fighting spirit. So let's share a laugh or two and make the journey an enjoyable one."

A letter sent after being rejected at the interview

April 22, 20__

Mr. Anthony Pierce, HR Manager
Winston Trails Industries International
5252 Newbury Street
Boston, MA 01999

Dear Mr. Pierce:

I am in receipt of your letter dated April 17th and thank you for your prompt response after our interview. I gave the letter much thought, and after careful consideration, I regret to inform you that I am unable to accept your rejection. I am certain you have made an error in judgment, and I wish to help you correct that error.

That being said, I believe we should schedule a time to discuss this within the week, as I would like a job offer by the end of the month. Truth be known, I have had many other cordial rejections. Given the great amount of competition I am up against, I find that, in good conscience, I can no longer accept all the rejections I am receiving.

I am certain Winston Trails Industries has an outstanding reputation for rejecting hundreds of candidates a week (not to mention all those candidates whose résumés don't make it through your firewalls or that simply get deleted). But I will consider myself the exception. FYI: I plan to begin work on May 2nd. I look forward to seeing you then.

Sincerely,

Randall C. Phillips

Winston Churchill said that *the natural state of the human experience is that of battle.* From the moment we're conceived, we battle to survive and thrive. The key, I think, is to learn how to battle better and enjoy the good times as well as the challenging times. Just like a symphony, life has its high and low notes. We don't go to the symphony to enjoy just the high happy parts of the performance. We sit and embrace the low and sad parts as well. This is what makes up the symphony, and this is what makes up life.

I, like you, was born without an owner's manual. Every day, I seek to find new answers to age-old questions in an effort to become a better warrior of life. It's been said that the greatest fear in life is not death. The greatest fear in life is what dies inside us while we live. So when negative and fearful emotions affect you in your pursuit of landing a new job in a troubled economy, master the art of battling life and career issues better. You can do this by asking more courageous questions to come up with innovative and practical answers. Manage your focus, and focus mostly on what you have rather than on what you don't have, because positive energy attracts positive results. Seek out others who have successfully overcome what you are facing, and determine what they did to achieve success. Then, do the same. And finally, never lose your sense of humor. It really is the best medicine that will put you on the road to your next job.

CHAPTER 1 SUMMARY: BEST WAYS 1–19

1. Develop a fearless constitution as a first step in landing a new job in troubled economic times.

2. Become an educated, enthusiastic, and confident campaigner to enable you to recover from job loss and land a new job in competitive job markets.

3. Change how you think about a job search—look at it as an easy five-step process that is a well-planned and well-executed campaign.

4. Allow yourself to be discomforted, as complacency and comfort are not catalysts for constructive change. It is discomfort that cures dis-ease.

5. Take personal responsibility for your future. Don't blame others or provide excuses. Adopt the belief that *if it's going to be, it's up to me!*

6. Invest 95 percent of your time and resources on the solution, not the problem.

7. Commit to identifying a meaningful goal, as all success is born out of a burning desire to achieve success.

8. Have faith. Faith is a feeling of certainty, that something good can be created even though it has yet to be determined when or how it will occur.

9. Work on building and improving your character. A healthy character comes from a sincere appreciation for all that you have today in pursuit of all that you want tomorrow.

10. Employ massive amounts of discipline. Discipline means doing what you don't want to do to get the job you want at the pay you deserve.

11. Surround yourself with positive and empowering people. In most cases, the people you associate with determine how quickly you'll land a new job.

12. Accept and embrace adversity and failure. No one gets it right the first time. Massive failure leads to massive success.

13. Work hard on your fitness and health. Landing a new job in troubled times requires a lot of energy. Eat well and exercise regularly to give yourself the energy you'll need to secure a new, rewarding job.

14. Take massive action. Action, driven by discipline, is what propels the process of getting a new job quickly and effectively.

15. Ask courageous questions. Asking high-quality questions stimulates new thoughts. New, more empowered thoughts will lead to a new job.

16. Manage your focus. Focus on what you have to be grateful for and what's going well in your life. If you focus on the negative, you'll get negative results. If you focus on the positive, you'll get positive results. Are you focusing on the 90 percent who are employed or the 10 percent who are unemployed? What you focus on determines your mindset and how quickly you obtain that new job.

17. Reference others who have successfully dealt with and overcome what you are currently experiencing. By doing so, you find strength and hope, and learn specific strategies and concepts used by others so you too can effectively work through and resolve the issues you face.

18. Use humor to find emotional balance in your life while you pursue a new job. Laughter is the best medicine not only for health issues, but for all life's adversities including job loss and job dissatisfaction.

19. Learn how to more effectively battle life and the job campaign by first learning how to better manage your mindset, your emotions. The four techniques covered in this chapter teach you how!

DEFINING YOUR GOAL

IF YOU DON'T KNOW WHERE YOU'RE GOING, IT'S HARD TO GET THERE

Picture a boat with an engine on the back. Now visualize the boat as your life and the engine as your job or career. The purpose of the engine is to power the boat to go where you want the boat to go and to do all the things you want to do. Metaphorically speaking, the boat is your life, and the engine is your career. The purpose of your job is to empower your life so you can achieve all that you want to achieve in life. The problem is that most people spend the first 20 years or more of their lives preparing how to earn a living, not how best to design a life.

TWO IMPORTANT QUESTIONS

To better understand the problem, we need only go back to that infamous question we ask youngsters early on. At four years of age, the child is asked, "What do you want to be when you grow up?" As a result, the child's identity is directly related to what she does in the workplace, not what she does in life or who she becomes as a person.

So you begin your life's journey on the academic assembly line in preschool or kindergarten and then, for the next 12 to 16 years or more, you prepare for one thing—getting a job. Most of your time, from preschool through high school and college, is spent on the engine of the boat, not the boat itself. And truth be known, the question "What do you want to be when you grow up?" is so ingrained into your being, you wind up spending your entire life seeking that elusive answer to this question, even at the age of 50 or 60! I constantly have people come up to me and ask, "How do I determine my dream job?" I answer the question by asking two of my own: 1) what do you want to get *out* of life? and 2) what do you want to *give back* to life? In other words, what are your life dreams? Who do you want to become? What do you want to own? Whom do you want as friends? What do you want to achieve and accomplish? What do you want to give back to your community? How do you want to contribute in making this world a little bit better place when you leave than when you arrived? And how do you want to be remembered?

Survey after survey confirms that somewhere between 65 and 90 percent of workers are uninspired with, or downright dislike, their jobs. When asked, 8 out of 10 people claim they would quit their jobs if they won the lottery, and most feel that they are underpaid, overworked, and underappreciated in the workplace. However, those few people who seem genuinely happy and successful at their jobs are those who acknowledge that they work at jobs and careers that inspire their life's dreams and ambitions. They understand that the key to a full and rewarding life is to first identify what kind of life would be considered full and rewarding. They know how they want to live, what kind of person they want to become, and what dreams and desires they want to pursue and achieve. Simply stated, those people who are enjoying life's journey, regardless of the challenges they face along the way, know their values and have exciting goals they wish to achieve. Then, once defined, they identify career and job opportunities that will be a catalyst for attaining the life they have designed for themselves.

WHEN THE PROMISE IS CLEAR, YOU'LL PAY THE PRICE

Every ambition has its price. The truth is, you'll pay any price if your ambitions and goals are inspiring ones. Said differently, you'll do whatever it takes when you are passionate about and committed to your goals. And if you don't know what your life goals and ambitions are, you might consider becoming passionate about defining them.

Here's a fact that should grab your attention. *If you don't have ambitions and goals of your own, you'll be destined to spend your entire life working hard to help others achieve their ambitions and goals at the expense of your own.* Goals that are not clear are clearly not goals. What cannot be identified cannot be attained. So the starting place for helping you identify your next job or career opportunity is not by determining what kind of job you want to work at, but rather by determining what kind of life you envision for yourself and your family. Once that vision is clear and you are jazzed about attaining it, meaningful job and career options will appear.

THE FOUR UNIVERSAL TRUTHS

There are four universal truths related to determining what job opportunities would best provide you with the life you want:

1. As I noted previously, *there is no magic pill.* If there were, the majority of people would be taking the pill and living for the week, not the weekend.

2. *Vocational tests are not effective.* If tests were useful, most people would be graduating from high school and college knowing precisely what job and career options would best inspire their lives. If vocational tests actually worked, it would stand to reason that 65 to 90 percent of the working population would enjoy what they do rather than the other way around.

3. *If you are not working diligently on identifying what constitutes a quality life for you and your family, odds are no one else is working on this for you.* And if you are putting this off or ignoring what constitutes a quality life for you and your family, know that the *Law of Ignoring* will kick in. The Law of Ignoring says that whatever you ignore will, most likely, get worse in time. *If you want to live life on your terms and secure a job that provides the life you want, you have to make it happen.*

4. *You must make time and enjoy the process of introspection.* You must take the time to think, reflect, contemplate, and indulge in personal intro-spection. A Zen expression says that *if you're not willing to go within, you'll have to go without!* Breakthroughs and new ideas normally don't present themselves when you're watching television or engaged in diversionary activities such as video games. You need to find a tranquil and peaceful setting where you can allow your thoughts and emotions to soar. Isn't it interesting that one of the major abilities that characterizes human beings is the ability to think? Yet most people go to bed with the same thoughts they awoke with. *How can you create anything new tomorrow with the same thoughts you had yesterday?* You must take time out of every day to think, to engage in self-reflection. It takes only one new thought to manifest a life-changing breakthrough, one idea to go from broke to fortune, and one idea to go from unemployed to happily employed. But that one new thought won't happen by chance; it will happen as a result of investing time to journey within.

THE FIVE STEPS TO IDENTIFYING MEANINGFUL CAREER GOALS

In 1992 when I was fired by one of my best friends, I was 39 years old and going through a serious midlife crisis. I knew I had the potential to be successful. I worked hard; I had a good education and was raised in a loving family. I grew up in a wonderful town and had many close friends. So how is it that with all the gifts that had been bestowed upon me, I was a *satellite in the wrong orbit* at age 39? The answer, I discovered, was that I wasn't taught the five steps to identify the kind of job and career that would inspire me or my life. Once I learned these five steps, my life changed almost instantly!

This chapter will introduce you to the five steps that turned my life and career around. And these five steps have also worked successfully for thousands of people I have shared them with over the years. *Each step requires specific work assignments that I will ask you to do.* And as I lead you through these five steps, I'll do the assignments with you and use myself as an example. This way you will see how I went from clueless to clarity in discovering what career would best inspire my life. The five steps are:

1. Identify your signature life values.
2. Identify your signature career values.
3. Acknowledge activities and environments that interest you.
4. Evaluate current market opportunities.
5. Know the four global options using the Circle of Options model (see later in the chapter) to determine your long- and short-term career goals.

Step #1: Identify Your Signature Life Values

Values come from the heart and are immutable at the moment. Yes, they may change tomorrow, a month from now, or a year from now. But at this moment, *your signature values are something you feel so strongly about; they can't be changed or compromised. In fact, they determine how happy you are at any moment in your life.* And the word *signature* means that you have a hierarchy (a prioritized list) of values that are yours and yours alone. The only way you can find joy in life and in your career is to know what your signature values are and then to work hard living harmoniously with them. For instance, if you value health and are not healthy physically or emotionally, you can't be happy. If you value financial independence and are broke, you can't be happy. If you value a loving relationship and you are in a toxic and unhealthy one, you can't be happy. If you value peace of mind but experience constant stress, you can't be happy.

The challenge for most people is they simply aren't aware of their signature values. They don't know what makes them happy! When you drive a car and are holding the steering wheel, doesn't the steering wheel move back and forth continuously while the car is in motion even when you are going straight? The reason the steering wheel is always moving is because the car is always trying to go off course. If you don't continually move the steering wheel, you'll crash! The same is true for your life and your career. If you don't continually control the values that determine your happiness, you'll crash and burn emotionally! *Every emotion you feel, every decision you make, and every action you take is guided by your values.* And here's what's exciting about your values. Though you may have 20, 30, or more values, there are only about 6 to 8 that make up 90 percent of your happiness. This means that when you identify your top 6 to 8 values and place them in a hierarchy of importance, you will then know precisely what makes you happy. You can then begin the process of living your life in harmony with your signature values. And when you live life and work at a job that is properly aligned with your values, you can't believe the joy you'll get out of every day! Life becomes an exciting adventure. On the other hand, when you live life in conflict with your values, you'll be constantly stressed out and unhappy. Life becomes a daily struggle.

So this first assignment will help you determine your signature life values. As I said, I will do the assignments with you. Use me as an example, but understand that my signature values are mine. You have to determine yours because that's the only way you can be happy and live a fulfilling life and work at a meaningful job. And when you work on this first assignment, allow yourself to *feel* your values. This exercise requires very little thinking.

It does, however, require you to open your heart and emotions to what's really important to you. Do not spend time judging or analyzing your values. When you intellectualize your values, you allow your head to get in the way of your heart, and you'll wind up confused and in conflict. The key here is to allow your heart (your desires) to have its say. When you make intellectual decisions that are in conflict with your heart's desires, you'll make poor decisions and wind up saying, "My heart's not in this any more." Unhappiness and frustration will prevail. The message here is that you must trust your feelings and emotions and give yourself the gift of knowing those six to eight things that make you happy.

How do you determine your values? You do so by asking yourself the following question: "What's most important to me in my *life* that will make me happy and that will significantly enhance the quality of my life?"

Plan to invest at least two to three hours answering that question. Ideally, you should be in a tranquil, relaxed, and empowering environment. Get fired up, and allow no interruptions. Let yourself feel all those aspects of life that would make you happy, provide meaning, and bring joy to you and others. Then write them down. Below were my values in 1992 when, as I noted above, I was fired by one of my best friends. Remember, I hadn't a clue, at age 39, what I wanted to be when I grew up. Through this process I discovered the answer. And so can you! *Be sure and brainstorm (heartstorm, actually) your values, not mine.* Recall times when you were the happiest. What made you happy? Think of times when you weren't so happy. What would have made you happy during those times? Think about all this, and just write down your thoughts *without analyzing or judging them.*

Assignment: Stop and invest quality time answering the question, "What's most important to me in my *life* that will make me happy and that will significantly enhance the quality of my life?" In addition to listing my life values back in 1992, I've provided a detailed list of values to help you to come up with your own.

> **Your Life Values. What's most important to me in my *life* that will make me happy and that will significantly enhance the quality of my life?**
>
> JAY'S VALUES IN 1992
>
> Health, freedom, a loving relationship, financial independence, family, friends, adventure, tranquility, golf, significance, time, respect, a nice home, a meaningful career, integrity, spirituality, travel, achievement, contribution, the power to influence, personal growth, tolerance, honesty, compassion, healthy competition, and hard work

A Partial List of Life Values

Health and fitness	Independence	Love	Hard work
Leisure activities	Financial freedom	Security	A loving family
Good friends	Exciting activities	Peace of mind	Peace on earth
Helping others	Sports	Respect	Honesty
Time	Trustworthiness	Spirituality	Patience
A nice home	A good job	Travel	Achievement
Community giving	Leadership	Personal growth	Compassion
Creativity	Loyalty	Acceptance	Comfort
Competency	A sense of humor	Courage	Control
Order	Kindness	Wisdom	Persistence
Thoughtfulness	Silliness	Sexuality	Recognition

Did you take the time to identify your life values? If you are reading this now, I assume you have responded to the question and now have your own list of values. Did you discover any surprises or breakthroughs? When

I created my list in 1992, I was most surprised by my values of *significance* and *the power to influence*. I must admit, I wasn't even aware of them! And because I was living my life without these two values, this caused quite a bit of pain in my life. So I hope you invested a good amount of time on determining what makes you happy, because if you don't know what brings you joy, how can you ever expect to be happy?

The Hierarchy

Now it's time to look at your list of life values and identify your top eight. *Then, you will prioritize them in the order of importance that naturally makes you happy. In other words, when you look at your hierarchy, it should feel great!* Prioritizing your values, or placing them in a hierarchy, allows you to better understand why you think the way you think, feel the way you feel, and act the way you act. Though all eight values are extremely important, some are a little more important than others. For instance, my eyesight is a little more important to me than my hearing, but that doesn't mean my hearing isn't important. By realizing this, I understand now why I'd be a bit more excited about going to a movie than a concert. I now understand why, when someone gives me directions, I always want to see a map rather than be told where to go. *If I know my hierarchy of values, I'll make better decisions because I know better what to base those decisions on.*

If finding a loving relationship and securing a new job are values that are important to you, but deep down in your heart, a loving relationship is a bit more important than securing a new job, you'll probably allocate more of your energy and resources to finding a loving relationship than you will to securing a new job. Your signature values represent your personal guidance or navigational system that steers your emotions and your life. If you live in harmony with your signature values, you'll find a deep sense of happiness and personal fulfillment. If you don't, you open yourself up to constant pain, stress, and conflict.

Assignment: In the next exercise, you will prioritize your top eight signature values. Keep in mind that all eight are very important. But your #1 value will be a bit more important to you than your #2 value, and your #2 value will be a bit more important than your #3 value, and so on. *Once your values are in the proper hierarchy, you will have identified your signature life values.* Then you can begin to live your life and make decisions based on this hierarchy. It's the *only* way you can live a happy, joyful life.

What are the eight most important values that will make me happy in life and the hierarchy of importance that constitutes my signature values?

1.	( )	5.	( )
2.	( )	6.	( )
3.	( )	7.	( )
4.	( )	8.	( )

Jay's hierarchy of values in 1992

1.	A loving relationship	( )
2.	Freedom	( )
3.	Financial independence	( )
4.	A meaningful career	( )
5.	Significance	( )
6.	The power to influence	( )
7.	Family and friends	( )
8.	Health	( )

I expect that you have completed this assignment and now have your life values in a hierarchy of importance, just as I listed mine above back in 1992. *Your emotional state and the actions you take in life are determined by how well you live according to your priority or hierarchy of values.* So once again, I ask the question, did you discover any surprises or breakthroughs? When I put my values in the hierarchy above, I was most surprised that my values of a loving relationship and freedom came ahead of financial independence and a meaningful career, even though I was broke at the time and had no clue what I wanted to do for a living. *But you see, I didn't analyze or judge my hierarchy.* This is how I *felt,* so this is how it was!

Grade Your Values

Now that you know what makes you happy and in the hierarchy that feels right to you, it's time to evaluate how happy you presently are with each value. You will notice parentheses following each value. Once you have your values listed in the correct hierarchy (your signature life values), go back and grade each one (I used an A–F grading system) based on how you feel you are currently living your life in harmony with that value. As you can see by how I graded my values back in 1992, my life was somewhat of a challenge to say the least!

1.	A loving relationship	(F)
2.	Freedom	(B)
3.	Financial independence	(D)
4.	A meaningful career	(F)
5.	Significance	(C)
6.	The power to influence	(C)
7.	Family and friends	(C)
8.	Health	(C)

Analyze Your Grades, *Not* Your Values

After grading my values, I analyzed my grades. As I did, I realized that *there were things I could do immediately to improve some of my grades.* I could work on my health immediately by eating better and exercising more. That would instantly improve my grade from a C to a B. I could immediately improve my relationships with family members and friends just by making a more concerted effort to do so. I could instantly bring that C way up to a B+! And the power to influence could easily become an A *if I used the power to influence myself to work harder than ever to achieve a happier more meaningful life.* In fact, I had a breakthrough with my power-to-influence value. The breakthrough was that I got excited about using the power to influence to empower myself to define and achieve a purposeful career.

Though nothing tangible had yet occurred, I felt an adrenaline rush because I felt genuine hope and anticipation. My two lowest grades were my #1 value (a loving relationship) and my #4 value (a meaningful career). But I had another breakthrough! I discovered that if I could improve the grades for my #6, #7, and #8 values, I'd have a much better "report card," and, more important, I'd be much happier. *The breakthrough came when I discovered that if I were happier, I'd be in a better, more empowered position to address my relationship and career challenges.*

So I made the decision to be happier and *changed my grades.* Compare my original grades, with attention to life values #6, #7, and #8) with my new, more empowering grades:

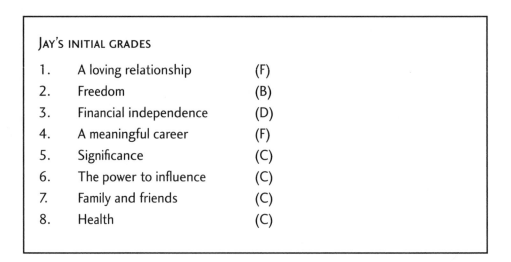

JAY'S INITIAL GRADES

1.	A loving relationship	(F)
2.	Freedom	(B)
3.	Financial independence	(D)
4.	A meaningful career	(F)
5.	Significance	(C)
6.	The power to influence	(C)
7.	Family and friends	(C)
8.	Health	(C)

JAY'S NEW, UPGRADED VALUES

1.	A loving relationship	(F)
2.	Freedom	(B)
3.	Financial independence	(D)
4.	A meaningful career	(F)
5.	Significance	(C)
6.	The power to influence	**(A)**
7.	Family and friends	**(B+)**
8.	Health	**(B)**

The power behind this exercise is to first identify your signature life values and then to evaluate them so you can better control how you feel about those values. *You do this by evaluating, grading, and then "upgrading" your level of happiness for each of your values when possible.* In other words, you can change your beliefs to find a higher degree of happiness to better address your challenges. I certainly had 100 percent control over my health and my relationships with family members and friends, yet I gave myself a C. *By realizing I was not controlling what I could control—like my health, my relationships with family members and friends, and how best to utilize my power to influence—I immediately improved my grades (changed my beliefs) and seized the power I always had. By doing so, I instantly found a new level of happiness.* With this newfound level of happiness, I could more constructively and enjoyably address my two major challenges—my relationship and career issues.

If you are like most people, you'll find that, like me back in 1992, you are not controlling those aspects of your life you actually have control over and aren't fully appreciating those things that are actually going well in your life. Once you make some adjustments in how you manage your happiness by changing your beliefs and upgrading the actual happiness levels for those values you are currently undervaluing, you too can constructively and enjoyably address your major issues, such as landing a job in a troubled and highly competitive job market.

Assignment: At this time, please return to your hierarchy of eight signature life values and grade them. Once graded, go back and reevaluate each one and ask yourself if you can create a newfound level of happiness by upgrading some of your grades. By doing so, you will find a greater level of happiness and can better address your more pressing issues.

Values Will Shift and Change

Indeed, your life's values will constantly shift and change. If you find that special person and get married, you have a new value that will head toward the top of your hierarchy. If you have children and need to start saving for their college education, saving money may be a value that moves up your hierarchy while the values of adventure or leisure activities might slide down. If health is your #7 value and you are diagnosed with a serious health issue, health will, most likely, ascend from #7 to #1. Certainly getting healthy will supersede almost everything else on your list. Just like the steering wheel that continually moves back and forth to keep your car safely on the road, you must continually evaluate and "steer" your values so you can keep your life on track and on the right road. You must be prepared to review and revisit your values and hierarchy on a regular basis.

Step #2: Identify Your Signature Career Values

You will now use the exact same strategy that you used to determine your signature life values to identify and prioritize your signature career values. You will ask the same question but substitute the word *career* for *life*. Here's the question you will now ask yourself: "What's most important to me in my career or job that will make me happy and that will significantly enhance the quality of my life?"

Once again, you will want to invest at least two to three hours on this assignment. I will provide you with my career values back in 1992 as I did with my life values. I remind you that my signature career values are, most likely, different from yours. So be sure to spend quality time identifying what makes you happy in a job or career. This is your future you are designing!

Assignment: Stop and invest quality time answering the question, "What's most important to me in my *career or job* that will make me happy and that will significantly enhance the quality of my life?" In addition to listing my specific career values back in 1992, I've provided a detailed list of career and job values to help you to come up with your own. Recall times when you were the happiest in a job or career. What made you happy? Think of times when you weren't that happy. What would have made you happier during those times? Think about all those things that would constitute the perfect job or work environment, and just write them down without analyzing or judging them.

What's most important to me in my *career or job* that will make me happy and that will significantly enhance the quality of my life?

JAY'S CAREER VALUES IN 1992

Writing, creativity, diversity, freedom, training people, helping others, being an industry leader, multiple streams of income, financial independence, respect, set my own schedule, travel, the power to influence, personal growth, and healthy competition

---

A Partial List of Career Values

Competitive environment	Supervise others	Earn a lot of money
High social status	Job security	Artistic expression
Independence	Problem solving	Leadership
Improve the environment	Friendships	Advancement
Physical challenge	Location of work	Short commute

Fast-paced environment	Work alone	Work in teams
Work with information	Work with data	Work with ideas
Change society for the better	Flexible schedule	No weekend work
Contact with the public	Recognition	Minimal stress
Precision work	Invent or create	Learning new things
Variety and change	Constant challenge	Structure
Adventure and excitement	Honesty and integrity	Power or authority
A good boss	A reputable company	A big corporation
A small company	Travel	Help society

I sincerely hope you put quality time into this important assignment. You can't be happy in a job when you don't know precisely what makes you happy. You should now have a comprehensive list of your career values.

Assignment: Now, as you did with your life values, you'll want to identify your top eight career values and then place them in a hierarchy of importance. Remember, when you define your signature career values, you begin the almost miraculous process of taking control of your future because you will be crystal clear on what has to happen for you to be happy in your next job! Only then can you identify, pursue, and land an enjoyable and rewarding job quickly and effectively.

What are the eight most important values that will make me happy in my *career* and the hierarchy of importance that constitutes my signature values?

1.   ( )
2.   ( )
3.   ( )
4.   ( )
5.   ( )
6.   ( )
7.   ( )
8.   ( )

JAY'S HIERARCHY OF VALUES IN 1992		
1.	Freedom	(F)
2.	Helping others	(F)
3.	Writing	(B)
4.	Financial independence	(D)
5.	Training people	(C)
6.	Industry leadership	(F)
7.	Creativity	(C)
8.	Multiple streams of income	(D)

Grade Your Last Job(s)

Since this exercise will be pivotal in helping you define those qualities that will make you happy in your next job or career, I hope you put a good amount of time and thought into this exercise. Did you come up with any breakthroughs? Did anything surprise you? When I put my values in the hierarchy above, I was most surprised that my top three out of four values were Fs and a D. And five of my eight values were either Fs or Ds. And as hard as I tried, I was *unable* to upgrade any of them. That being said, I studied my hierarchy of career values and the grades I gave them. Then I thought to myself, "There's little wonder why I had no passion for my job and got myself fired. As I look back on this job, I realize that my good friend did me a *big* favor by firing me!"

Assignment: Please return to your signature career values and grade them. Then go back and reevaluate them, and ask yourself if you can create a new-found level of happiness by upgrading some of your grades. By doing this, you can begin the process of addressing those other values that need to be addressed to help you select job or career options that inspire you.

Assignment: At this point, you should have identified *both* your signature life and signature career values. This will allow you to make quality decisions about future job and career options. Before we move on to Step #3, let's put your signature life and career values together for future reference just as I did.

Jay's Life and Career Values

My Eight Life Values

1.   A Loving relationship
2.   Freedom
3.   Financial independence
4.   A meaningful career
5.   Significance
6.   The power to influence
7.   Family and friends
8.   Health

My Eight Career Values

1.   Freedom
2.   Helping others
3.   Writing
4.   Financial independence
5.   Training people
6.   Industry leadership
7.   Creativity
8.   Multiple streams of income

Your Life and Career Values

My Eight Life Values

1.   _____
2.   _____
3.   _____
4.   _____
5.   _____
6.   _____
7.   _____
8.   _____

MY EIGHT CAREER VALUES

1. _____
2. _____
3. _____
4. _____
5. _____
6. _____
7. _____
8. _____

Step #3: Acknowledge Jobs and Industries That Interest You

When you explore new job and career options, you need only define 1) *jobs that would interest you,* that you are or could be qualified to do, and that are in harmony with your career and life values and 2) *industries that interest you.* The T-Bar model is a self-brainstorming tool to help you answer the question, "What do I want to do?" On one side of the "T," you'll list jobs. On the other, you'll list industries.

Example

POTENTIAL JOBS	POTENTIAL INDUSTRIES
Computer programmer	Health care
Sales professional	Entertainment
IT consultant	Sports
Trainer or technical trainer	Technology environments
Technical writer	High-end automotive
Technical troubleshooter	Music industry and venues
Animation or movie director	
Musician	

Assignment: Using the T-Bar model, complete your next assignment by writing down all the jobs and industries that would interest you. At this time and with *very little thought*, write down all the different jobs that you would enjoy on the left side of the T-Bar. On the right side, list all the industries you would be interested in working in. *Write everything down no matter how ridiculous it might seem at first. Be innovative, bold, and honest with yourself! You can always delete your ideas later.* Consider those jobs and industries you have enjoyed in the past. Also, write down ones you've always dreamt about. What jobs or industries would turn you on? *What jobs or industries would be so enjoyable that your weekdays would actually be more exciting than your weekends?* Prepare to invest a good amount of time on this assignment. Don't leave anything off this list. If an idea comes to you, write it down! When done, place the items in a hierarchy where the most exciting jobs and industries are atop the list. My list, from 1992, is below.

Jay's T-Bar in 1992

POTENTIAL ACTIVITIES	POTENTIAL ENVIRONMENTS
1. Writer	1. Sports
2. Trainer	2. Employment or job management
3. Speaker or presenter	3. Motivation and empowerment
4. Marketing and communications	4. Tourism
5. Manager	5. Business consulting
6. Adventure guide (tourism)	

Now is the time for you to brainstorm your own list. (By the way, if you find that you need a comprehensive resource to further assist you, the U.S. Department of Labor has identified over 30,000 specific job titles that are available in its publication *The Dictionary of Occupational Titles*.)

Your T-Bar

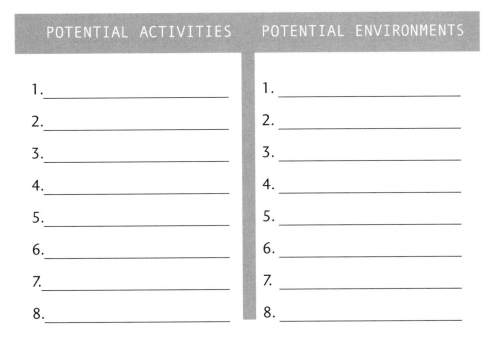

POTENTIAL ACTIVITIES   POTENTIAL ENVIRONMENTS

1. _____ 1. _____
2. _____ 2. _____
3. _____ 3. _____
4. _____ 4. _____
5. _____ 5. _____
6. _____ 6. _____
7. _____ 7. _____
8. _____ 8. _____

Step #4: Evaluate Current Market Opportunities

No doubt, you'd certainly have a challenging time landing a job as a snow-plow operator in Florida or getting a job as a pay-phone repair person at a time when almost everyone has a cell phone. But even in troubled economies, there are many job opportunities and almost unlimited ways to earn a good income. You just have to know what they are. *Study the job market where you live or where you are seeking work. You must know what jobs and industries are on the rise and those on the decline.* Conduct your own in-depth research online. Enter the keywords "growth industries," and specify your geographic area. Read newspapers, including the business section as well as the classified section. Pay attention to what's going on in your market; speak to businesspeople you might know or to professionals at the Workforce One-Stops. Visit your local chamber of commerce, and ask employees there what market opportunities are growing. Another source of market information can be provided by executive recruiters. Take an executive recruiter out to lunch, and get his or her take on the job market. Ask everyone and anyone you can about what jobs are hot and what are not. And once you have performed an in-depth study of your market, write down the top six to eight jobs and industries that currently provide the best opportunities.

In 1992 when I was fired from my job, the U.S. economy was just working its way out of a severe recession. The unemployment rate in Florida, where I lived, was 8.9 percent. Many industries that drove Florida's economy were struggling, including tourism, real estate, construction, finance, and food and beverage. I performed a detailed job market analysis and identified growth jobs and emerging industries. I've included them in the list below:

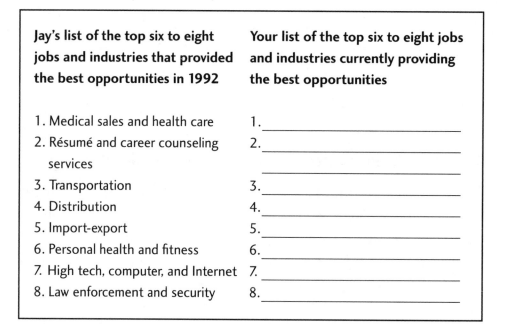

Jay's list of the top six to eight jobs and industries that provided the best opportunities in 1992	Your list of the top six to eight jobs and industries currently providing the best opportunities
1. Medical sales and health care	1. _____
2. Résumé and career counseling services	2. _____ _____
3. Transportation	3. _____
4. Distribution	4. _____
5. Import-export	5. _____
6. Personal health and fitness	6. _____
7. High tech, computer, and Internet	7. _____
8. Law enforcement and security	8. _____

Assignment: Your next assignment is to perform a job market analysis in your area so you know which specific jobs and industries to consider. Take time to perform the appropriate due diligence and gather information that will help you identify all growth and emerging industries. Once you have completed this, you can better select the right job and industry for you. Then, list the information in the spaces above.

Step #5: Know the Four Global Options Using the Circle of Options Model

At this point, you should have a substantial amount of information to help you make a decision about what new career direction would be best for you. When you know your life and career values, you have identified the jobs and industries you'd like to work in, and you have a grasp of current market opportunities, you can use this information to select viable career options like pieces of a puzzle. You may very well come up with both long- and short-term goals. For instance, you may decide that the long-term goal is to become an office manager for a medical practice. The short-term goal may be to secure a part-time job for six months while you take computer classes and a financial accounting class that will give you the added skills and qualifications needed to land a job as an office manager.

Assignment: At this time, you will put all the pieces to the career puzzle together in one place. This way, you'll have the information readily available so you can see the *BIG* picture in order to make *BIG* decisions. Please do this now!

Your Life and Career Values

MY EIGHT LIFE VALUES

1. _____
2. _____
3. _____
4. _____
5. _____
6. _____
7. _____
8. _____

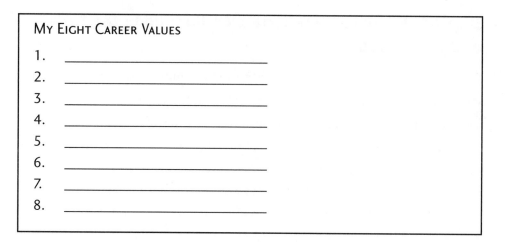

MY EIGHT CAREER VALUES

1. _____
2. _____
3. _____
4. _____
5. _____
6. _____
7. _____
8. _____

Your T-Bar

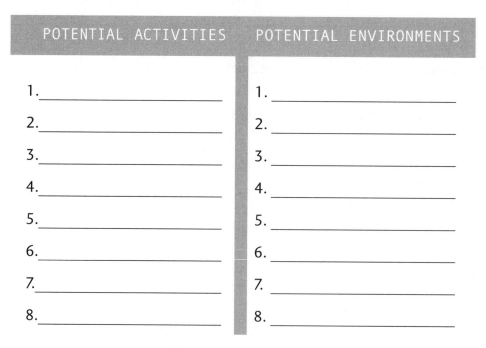

POTENTIAL ACTIVITIES	POTENTIAL ENVIRONMENTS
1._____	1. _____
2._____	2. _____
3._____	3. _____
4._____	4. _____
5._____	5. _____
6._____	6. _____
7._____	7. _____
8._____	8. _____

Six to Eight Jobs and Industries That Currently Provide Employment Opportunities

1. _____
2. _____

3. _____

4. _____

5. _____

6. _____

7. _____

8. _____

Notes, reflections, and breakthroughs:

_____

Jay's Life and Career Values

My Eight Life Values

1.   A Loving relationship
2.   Freedom
3.   Financial independence
4.   A meaningful career
5.   Significance
6.   The power to influence
7.   Family and friends
8.   Health

My Eight Career Values

1.   Freedom
2.   Helping others
3.   Writing
4.   Financial independence
5.   Training people
6.   Industry leadership
7.   Creativity
8.   Multiple streams of income

Jay's T-Bar in 1992

POTENTIAL ACTIVITIES	POTENTIAL ENVIRONMENTS
1. Writer	1. Sports
2. Trainer	2. Employment or job management
3. Speaker or presenter	3. Motivation and empowerment
4. Marketing and communications	4. Tourism
5. Manager	5. Business consulting
6. Adventure guide (tourism)	

Six to Eight Jobs and Industries That Provided Employment Opportunities in 1992

1. Medical sales and health-care positions—nurses, techs, and administrative jobs

2. Employment services including résumé writing and career coaching

3. Transportation—shipping, trucking, railroad, and planes

4. Distribution—warehouse management, shipping and receiving, traffic management

5. Import-export—sales, sourcing and purchasing, governmental and business liaisons

6.   Personal health and fitness

_____

7.   High tech, computer, and Internet

_____

8.   Law enforcement and security—public and private

_____

Notes, reflections, and breakthroughs: Through this process, I realized that I always enjoyed writing, speaking, and training. I also realized *that if I had problems identifying and securing a rewarding job or career, there must be many others out there in a similar situation.* This presented a unique opportunity, and so I focused on employment services (item 2) from the list above.

There are only four global options you have when considering a new job or career. Below, write down the job you last held or are working at currently. Then write down the industry you last worked in or are currently working in.

Job:

_____

Industry:

_____

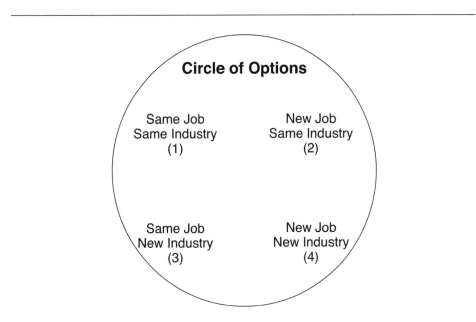

The Four Global Options

Now that you grasp the BIG picture, which includes your life values, your career values, your T-Bar, and current market conditions, it's time to consider the four global options. I call these global options because, in reality, these are the only four job or career options you have.

- *Option #1: Same job–same industry.* Choosing Option #1 means you enjoy both and, most likely, need only conduct a job transition campaign to seek out a new company or organization. For example, a fifth grade teacher who is teaching in a public school may seek the same job (teacher) in the same industry (public school system); this teacher only needs to look at a new school in the same school district or to apply for a teacher's position in a new school district.

- *Option #2: New job–same industry.* Option #2 means you enjoy the industry but need to identify a new job within that industry. Using the fifth grade teacher as an example again, she might seek a new job as an assistant principal or librarian. Or maybe she wants to earn more money than she would make as a teacher, so she becomes a sales professional and sells textbooks to educational institutions. The job transition campaign will take place within education, but she will identify and pursue a new, more inspiring, and more rewarding job within that industry.

- *Option #3: Same job–new industry.* If you select Option #3, it means you enjoy your job or vocation, but you need to identify a new industry or environment to perform that job in. The fifth grade teacher might get a job teaching for a private school (new industry or venue) or a private learning center, or she might even start her own tutoring business. In this case, the job transition campaign will focus on teaching but in a new, more appealing industry or venue.

- *Option #4: New job–new industry.* This option means you are ready for a wholesale change. Oftentimes this option is the option of choice if there's a career or job you've always dreamt about. Or possibly you have a nice severance package or the financial means to return to school and prepare for an entirely new career. Possibly the fifth grade teacher always had a passion for antiques. In this case, she might pursue a job as a manager or even an owner of an antique store. Perhaps she'll make the decision to stay home and be a full-time mom. The job transition campaign will focus on an entirely new job or activity in an entirely new industry or venue.

What Is Your Preference—Your Gut Instinct?

_____

_____

How I Came to Make My Decision

When I was fired in 1992, I held the job of marketing director for a company in the automotive aftermarket industry. I spent an entire weekend reviewing and evaluating my values, my T-Bar, the job market, and my four global options. It took me about four hours before I selected Option #3, *same job in a new industry*. I discovered that I enjoyed marketing because it integrated many of my career values, including writing, creativity, and training. However, I was a fish out of water in the automotive industry. This was not the industry for me.

Then I had a major breakthrough! *My heart was aching for a marketing job that would satisfy my career value of helping others. My brain went to work and came up with a life-changing idea. Why not use my talents and passions to market people?* In other words, why not use my marketing skills to help people market themselves in competitive job markets? I could become the Madison Avenue marketing expert for promoting people. I would assist individuals to effectively identify, pursue, and secure jobs they wanted. I figured that companies and organizations hire professional marketers to package and position their products and services for competitive markets, so why wouldn't individuals hire a professional marketer to package and position them for competitive job markets? *This idea felt right. For the first time in my life, I felt this is what I was meant to do! I was excited and became totally committed to this goal.*

A WORD ABOUT BRIDGING

Bridging is a term used to describe a multistep process of going from where you are to where you want to be. A doctor has to take multiple bridges before she can become a licensed physician. She has to travel on the undergraduate bridge for 4 years. Next she needs to cross the medical school bridge for another 4 years. Then there's the residency bridge, internship bridge, and possibly a fellowship bridge to cross. She has more than 10 years of "bridging" to do before she becomes a licensed physician!

I had to spend five years on the "get-to-know-your-new-industry bridge," studying everything I could about career and job management. I attended as many training courses as I could and met as many industry leaders as possible. I also worked three years writing my own book and helped create the first-ever professional résumé writing and career coaching association. But I also had to make a living. So I had to also cross the "résumé writing bridge." I began writing résumés as marketing tools rather than as assembly-line, look-alike biographies. I formed my own company because freedom is my top career value, and I defined freedom as working for myself.

I have to admit, I met a lot of resistance along the way. Some family members insisted I was unrealistic. One close friend doubted I could actually make a living writing résumés while I prepared to become an executive career coach. When I began writing my first book in 1994, one naysayer told me I had a better chance of going to the moon than getting a book published!

The most important lesson I learned back then was that anything was possible if I was committed to it. This is a valuable lesson for you. Anything is possible for you if you are committed to your goal. You must not give anyone permission to rob you of your dreams or let anything get in the way of attaining your true potential.

I DON'T HAVE THE MONEY TO ACHIEVE MY DREAMS

When I was terminated in 1992, I had no money, no savings, and no idea what I wanted to do for a living. But I had studied too many people who went from poverty to millionaire and billionaire, including Oprah, Sylvester Stallone, JC Penney, Colonel (Harland) Sanders, Henry Ford, and Ray Kroc, the man who transformed McDonald's into an international household word. Now that I had an exciting goal to become a marketing consultant for people, *I knew that my success depended less on what resources I had than how resourceful I could be.*

It didn't happen overnight. I worked long hours, met significant obstacles, and fell flat on my face more times than I care to remember. I found that rejection was a daily event that I had to learn to accept and deal with. On the other hand, I met some of the greatest people I've ever met in my life, including my soul mate (and that satisfied my #1 life value!). I helped many people secure jobs they otherwise would not have landed. And though it took longer than expected, by 1997 my dream of becoming a published author came true when McGraw-Hill offered me the first of what would be many book deals.

If I were to meet the friend who fired me back in 1992 today, I would thank him for that life-changing gift. Though I didn't know it then, he freed me to be able to identify and pursue my dreams. *Whatever you are experiencing this minute is a gift in disguise, though it may not seem so at this moment.* Remember, you are guided by your values. Go back and make sure you have put 100 percent of your heart and soul into these assignments. Like a jigsaw puzzle, all the pieces are there. You just have to have the patience and discipline to put them together!

IF THE ANSWER DOESN'T COME TODAY OR TOMORROW

We didn't get to the moon in a week, a month, or a year. It took nearly 10 years to get there. And NASA experienced a number of setbacks and tragedies along the way. Just because the answers don't come today or tomorrow doesn't mean you stop pursuing them or quit on yourself and your family. Instant gratification is not a virtue; patience and persistence are. Be innovative, resourceful, and relentless in pursuit of identifying a career that will inspire an extraordinary life.

ENTREPRENEURIALISM

Entrepreneurialism just may be the route many job seekers will have to explore today if the job market remains as competitive and volatile as it is. Indeed, entrepreneurialism is what made this country great. And there is no doubt that troubled economies normally produce high rates of unemployment. As we head into the second decade of the twenty-first century, the industrial complex and overall production capabilities in the United States are on the decline. When the cold war ended, approximately two billion people around the world were poised to enter the free market system and embrace capitalism. *Today, half the world's workers earn less than $3 a day!* Not surprisingly, then, outsourcing and global competition won't go away. Literally billions of people are just beginning to climb the capitalist ladder that Americans began climbing more than 200 years ago. Healthy, global competition will only expand and intensify. So when facing a tight job market, one option to consider is entrepreneurialism—full or part time.

And technology, within the borders of the United States, is having an even greater impact on job loss than outsourcing or immigration challenges. ATMs are replacing tellers, self-service checkout technologies are replacing cashiers, and robots are replacing technicians. At a time where mass layoffs are taking place in so many sectors of society, where will future jobs come from? Will job security ever come back? What new industries will spring up tomorrow to provide jobs for the millions of people who are being let go today? Entrepreneurialism may be the answer for many.

Profits May Be Better Than Wages

Until new, yet-to-be-defined industries emerge to accommodate the millions of people who are out of work, many may have no choice but to turn to self-employment—entrepreneurialism—as a solution to unemployment. For many, profits will replace wages. For others, becoming an independent contractor will replace becoming an employee. Think about this seriously, for a moment. If you spend three to six months to finally land a new job, what guarantees do you have that you won't wind up with the "boss from hell," who will force you to quit or terminate you? What guarantees do you have that a merger won't occur, that bankruptcy won't be filed, or that some other situation won't arise that will lead to yet another job loss? How many times will you opt to invest six months or more in landing a job that might not last very long?

When you can no longer depend on companies and organizations for your family's financial well-being and security, you'll have to take matters into your own hands. This is not the place to discuss the intricacies of starting and managing a business enterprise, be it a one-person painting company or a national franchise. But this is a good time to get you to start thinking about it. As the economy and job market adjust to the new realities of global competition, machines replacing people and world events that affect day-to-day life (such as 9/11), you may want to think about entrepreneurial and independent contracting opportunities. Whether you work at your own business full- or part-time, become an independent contractor, purchase an existing business, start up your own venture, open a home-based Internet business, or partner with others, entrepreneurialism (self-sufficiency) may be the last best hope for providing a steady income for you and your family. No doubt, there are risks to this option, and so the entrepreneurial alternative must be studied and researched very carefully. But if job security is anywhere on your list of values, you just might discover that the best chance you have of satisfying that value is to put your future in your own hands, not those of an employer.

MULTIPLE JOBS AND INCOME SOURCES

From my early teens through college, I always worked at multiple jobs. I had two paper routes, mowed lawns, shoveled snow, worked construction, labored in a leather factory, was a store detective, worked summers as a camp counselor, pumped gas (before technology eliminated that job), and sold greeting cards, just to name a few! I always had multiple income sources. Even if I was terminated from a job, it never affected me because I always had plenty of other ways to earn money.

Then, when I completed college, I bought into the idea that I should put all my eggs in one basket. In other words, once I graduated from college, I allowed myself and my family to be at the mercy of one employer. I purchased a home and took out a mortgage. I purchased an automobile and took out a car loan. I suddenly began to live in fear because, for the first time in my life, I had placed my financial security and well-being in the hands of one source, one company, one boss. Does this make any sense to you? I was told how many sick days and vacation days I was entitled to. I was told what insurance plan I qualified for. I was told how to dress. I was sent to training seminars on how to speak and act the way the company wanted me to speak and act. I was told when I had to work late, over weekends, and during my vacation—whether I liked it or not.

I never experienced financial stress prior to graduating from college because I had multiple income sources. After I completed college, I experienced nothing but stress. By age 26, I reverted to my successful model of multiple income sources. I figured either I could watch TV and make others rich, or I could spend evenings working on different ways to earn extra money and make myself rich! I chose earning money and creating my own security over watching television.

How about you? Are you ready to roll up your sleeves and take control over your financial future? You might opt to weave multiple part-time jobs together rather than rely on one employer. Perhaps you'll choose to supplement a full-time job with a part-time position. The main message here is that security may have to be redefined as "taking care of yourself rather than putting your life and the welfare of your family in the hands of others." Being an entrepreneur and creating multiple streams of income can be exciting and highly rewarding options if you think it out properly and go about it strategically.

In any case, it is vital to recognize that the U.S. economy and job market are going through an unprecedented time in human history. *The world has always been in a state of change, but today, with the onslaught of technological advances, what used to take 60 years to change now changes in about 60 hours!* Indeed, the price of gasoline alone changes every few minutes! Human beings, for the most part, are creatures of habit and feel comfortable operating in their comfort zone. They don't particularly embrace change. *And yet today, those who will survive and thrive in the new economy will be those who embrace, prepare for, and adapt to change.*

You may have to turn off the TV and head back to the classroom on a regular basis to attain new skills and knowledge so you don't become *worth less* to the marketplace. You may have to work nights and weekends at multiple jobs to maintain the quality of life you aspire to. You may need to consider moving and relocating more often to venues (national and international) that offer more lucrative employment opportunities. All this is neither good nor bad; it is what it is. But let me remind you that today anything is possible. *You live in a time where extraordinary opportunities are available every day to good, hardworking individuals who are prepared for change.* When you know your values, have inspiring goals, and are willing to go the extra mile because you know it's the best investment you can make in your future, you will begin the liberating process of creating employment opportunities that you enjoy and that inspire your whole life!

CHAPTER 2 SUMMARY: BEST WAYS 20–45

20. You must first acknowledge that the purpose of your job or career is to empower your life so you can achieve all that you want to achieve in life.

21. Ask the two most important life questions in order to live a full and rewarding life: 1) what do you want to get *out* of life? and 2) what do you want to *give back* to life?

22. The starting place for helping you identify your next job or career opportunity is not by determining what kind of job you want to work at, but rather by determining what kind of life you envision for yourself.

23. You must determine your signature values because this is the only way you can be happy, live a fulfilling life, and work at a meaningful job.

24. Values, unlike beliefs, come from the heart, not the head. When you identify your signature values, you will do very little thinking. You will allow your heart to feel what makes you happy.

25. To determine your life values, ask the question, "What's most important to me in my *life* that will make me happy and that will significantly enhance the quality of my life?"

26. To determine your signature life values, you must identify your top eight values and prioritize them in the order of importance that naturally makes you happy.

27. Prioritize your values, because when you know your hierarchy, you'll make better decisions based on this prioritized list.

28. Once you have established your life values, grade them individually according to how happy you are living life in harmony with them. By doing so, you will have a clear understanding of what you have to work on to live a rich and rewarding life.

29. Control what you can control. Evaluate your grades, and then upgrade wherever possible. This will help raise your level of happiness so that you may better address the more pressing issues.

30. Understand that your life's values will constantly shift and change. You must be prepared to review and revisit your values and hierarchy on a regular basis.

31. To determine your career values, ask the question, "What's most important to me in my *career* that will make me happy and that will significantly enhance the quality of my life?"

32. To determine your signature career values, you must identify your top eight values and prioritize them in the order of importance that naturally makes you happy.

33. Prioritize your career values, because when you know your hierarchy, you'll make better decisions since you'll know better what to base your career and job decisions on.

34. Once you have established your career values, grade them individually according to how happy you are or were working in harmony with them. By doing so, you will have a clear understanding of what you have to work on to identify a rich and rewarding job.

35. Control what you can control. Evaluate your grades (for your career values) and then upgrade those you can, just as you did with your life values. This way, you can better address the more pressing issues.

36. When you explore new job and career options, you need only define 1) jobs that would interest you, that you are qualified or wish to do, and that are in harmony with your career and life values and 2) industries that interest you. Use the T-Bar model to brainstorm jobs and industries that you would enjoy.

37. When you have completed working the T-Bar brainstorming exercise, place your list in a hierarchy where the most exciting jobs and industries are atop the list.

38. Study the job market where you live or where you are seeking work. You must know what jobs and industries are on the rise and those on the decline.

39. Once you have performed an in-depth study of your market, write down the top six to eight jobs and industries that currently provide the best opportunities.

40. Put all the pieces to the career puzzle together in one place. This way, you'll have the information readily available so you can see the BIG picture in order to make BIG decisions.

41. Use the Circle of Options model to determine if you want to work in the same job–same industry, new job–same industry,

same job–new industry, or new job–new industry. These are the only four global options you have.

42. Use the technique of *bridging* to go from where you are to where you want to be. This is used when you determine that it will require multiple steps to get there.

43. Don't ever quit on your dreams or settle for less than you can be. If you don't come up with the answers the first time around, go back and redo the assignments in this chapter. Just because the answers don't come today doesn't mean they won't come tomorrow or sometime next week. But one thing is for certain. If you do quit on your dreams, they will never have a chance!

44. Consider entrepreneurialism—becoming an independent contractor or consultant as a career option. Profits may be better than wages. At a time where there is little job security, the best job security may be that which you provide for yourself.

45. Create multiple streams of income. It may not be the best strategy to put all your eggs in one basket; in one employer. To protect yourself, your family, and your financial future, consider multiple income sources.

USING VALUE-BASED RÉSUMÉS AND SELF-MARKETING TOOLS

AVERAGE RÉSUMÉS WON'T ATTRACT OUTSTANDING JOBS

THE VALUE-BASED RÉSUMÉ

In a troubled economy plagued with high unemployment and employee dissatisfaction in the workplace, look-alike, assembly-line résumés won't get the attention of hiring authorities. Hiring authorities, including human resource professionals, executive recruiters, and hiring managers, don't have time to read stacks of boring biographies from strangers. They want to know quickly what specific contributions you can make and results you can produce. So, by definition, *a value-based résumé is a marketing document that communicates your ability to produce significant results better than other qualified candidates.*

You have 100 percent control over what you include in your résumé and how you present your marketing document. Unfortunately, most job seekers don't take advantage of their power to control the information that hiring authorities need to see on candidates' résumés. When you effectively control the information on your résumé, you will elicit attention and enthusiasm from prospective employers and win an interview. *More than 98 percent of the résumés being circulated today are nothing more than chronological obituaries,* biographies prepared on white paper with black ink and formatted like millions of others. Not only do they all look alike, they also don't communicate enough to differentiate themselves from other competing candidates. Most résumés don't address prospective employers' needs, problems, or organizational objectives. They don't shout out why they are the best candidate for the job. *During tough economic times, there are way too many competing résumés in circulation for you to submit a blend-in-with-everyone-else résumé. Your résumé must STAND OUT if you have any chance of attracting outstanding job opportunities.* Your résumé must be reader-friendly yet powerful in its messages. Your résumé must be exciting and professional, and be a document that you are proud of. In the end, your résumé must effectively promote and sell you to prospective employers. And especially in a troubled economy, you must promote and sell yourself better than other candidates who are going after the same jobs that you want!

A value-based résumé offers a number of specific advantages such as the following:

1. *Market value.* The process of creating a value-based résumé will result in your being able to effectively identify and communicate your value to prospective employers. Your résumé will clearly communicate bottom-line results and organizational contributions you can produce that position you as a highly qualified and valuable candidate.

2. *Differential factor.* When you strategically develop your value-based résumé, you will define the differential factor. The differential factor represents highly valuable skills, qualifications, and other employment assets that set you apart from other qualified candidates, that make you STAND OUT. Oftentimes, the differential factor is what tips the hiring scale in your favor! For instance, if you have an industry-wide reputation, your reputation might be the differential factor. If you are a black belt in Six Sigma, that may constitute the differential factor. A number of years ago, I coached a chief financial officer who worked for a legendary golf professional. Having worked for a famous golf professional was

the differential factor because many hiring managers found it unique and intriguing to interview (and hire) someone who worked for a celebrity. Perhaps you are bilingual; this may represent the differential factor. When you identify the differential factor, you'll provide your job campaign with a distinct advantage in landing a job quickly in the toughest of job markets.

3. *Confidence builder.* When you design and create a value-based résumé that communicates your value and those attributes that set you apart from your competition, you gain a whole new level of confidence in yourself, your ability to promote yourself, and your ability to remain upbeat throughout the entire job campaign. You will be proud of what you are marketing—namely, you! You will approach each day with a renewed sense of self-worth, knowing that you truly STAND OUT from others seeking the same jobs you want.

4. *"Door opener."* Value-based résumés open the right doors. Exciting, well-presented, value-based résumés open doors of opportunity that otherwise would not open for you. Your résumé will race to the top of the pile because it bellows out to employers, "This is what I can do for you—why I am a good fit for your company and the best candidate for the job."

5. *Stronger, more effective interviewee.* Value-based résumés lead to interviews, and interviews lead to job offers. When you write your résumé thinking about the interview, you begin developing the key messages you'll eventually want to communicate in an interview to win the job. In other words, when you take the time to properly prepare your résumé thinking about the key messages that will win job offers, you'll then showcase those messages on your résumé to win interviews!

Rules for Writing Value-Based Résumés

There are no rules! The goal of your résumé is to STAND OUT from your competition and to get prospective employers excited about the prospects of interviewing and hiring you. Rules mean conformity. How can you STAND

OUT or distinguish yourself from other job candidates if you blend in with them? Coca-Cola doesn't package itself to look like Pepsi. Tylenol doesn't package itself to look like Excedrin. Ford doesn't package itself to look like Toyota. And you shouldn't package yourself to look like your competition.

Of course, there are a number of guidelines I might suggest, especially during troubled times and oversaturated job markets. Next I've listed 12 guidelines for you to consider. But in the end, you have to think hard about what strategy will work most effectively for you. Then, execute it.

- *Guideline #1: Make your case in 15 to 20 seconds or less.* Most hiring authorities claim they spend 15 to 20 seconds, at most, reviewing your résumé to determine if they want to read more of your document and invite you in for an interview. In that 15-to–20-second window of opportunity, you must communicate your value, showcasing and head-lining those qualities that ring out, "I'm a highly qualified candidate worthy of a closer look!"

- *Guideline #2: Keep the résumé as brief as possible.* Today, given the myriad of voices vying for attention and the scores of résumés that are crossing the desks of hiring authorities, shorter is better. A solid one- or two-page résumé is the norm, but not without exception. If you have a *strategic reason* to write a résumé longer than one or two pages, by all means do so. But be careful not to conduct the interview in the résumé or ask the reader to labor through pages and pages of "stuff." Be precise and on message, and keep your résumé as brief as possible.

- *Guideline #3: Remember for whom you are writing the résumé.* In most cases, you're writing your résumé for a stranger who doesn't know you at all. Your main objective is to understand what prospective employers are looking for and then to provide that information clearly on your résumé. Do prospective employers want to read your biography, or do they prefer to know how you can contribute to their organizational goals? Before you write your résumé, seek first to understand the needs of potential employers, and then communicate, on your résumé, how you can best meet those needs.

- *Guideline #4: Résumés without achievements are like report cards without grades.* Hiring authorities and prospective employers know that a key indicator of future performance is past performance. It's not what you did in the past that determines your "hireability"; it's the results and achievements you produced that matters most. Your résumé is not the place to be humble! It's the place to professionally and confidently show off your past achievements and blow your own horn—loud and clear!

- *Guideline #5: Select your vocabulary with meticulous care.* Did you increase sales or *orchestrate explosive growth in revenues?* Did you provide good levels of customer service or *unparalleled levels of quality customer service?* As a receptionist, did you merely greet people, or were you *the manager of first impressions?* Are you a good problem solver, or can you *resolve complex technical issues professionally and expeditiously?* Words are power, and keywords and phrases are powerful agents for eliciting the right emotions to enthusiastically engage prospective employers to want to read your document. Well-chosen words can be the difference between an interview and a missed opportunity, so select your words and messages with painstaking precision.

- *Guideline #6: Be sure the résumé is well organized and reader-friendly.* It won't help much if you have extraordinary skills and qualifications but a hiring manager is unable to access the information. Take care not to use many different fonts or bullets. Balance your information with white space so the document is pleasant to read. You might want to limit the use of italics, as information presented in italics is normally difficult to read. The presentation should be crisp, exciting, and inviting. If you can't get totally jazzed about your résumé, how do you expect a potential employer to?

- *Guideline #7: Be professionally innovative and different.* Yes, you can use pictures, graphics, and graphs on your résumé. Yes, you can use color, shading, and boxes so messages JUMP OFF THE PAGE! Yes, you can include short references or testimonials within the résumé itself. That being said, you must know your audience and play to their emotions and expectations. Some forums still require a more traditional presentation. Be as bold and innovative as you can without coming across as gimmicky or amateurish. Be confidently courageous and professionally astute.

- *Guideline #8: Test-market your résumé.* When you have completed writing your résumé, identify five to seven people whose opinions you value and ask for their honest feedback. You may want to show it to a human resource manager, an executive recruiter, or an English teacher. Ask these five to seven people if you left anything important out or if there is something that needs to be deleted. Have them look for any lingering typos or grammatical errors. When you have five to seven sets of eyes review your résumé, chances are you'll end up with a perfectly constructed document that you can be proud of and that will do you proud!

- *Guideline #9: Address potential problems on the résumé.* Indeed, this breaks with traditional "rules." During troubled times and in high unemployment economies, many companies go out of business or reduce their labor force. As a result, possibly you've worked at many jobs in a short time frame where you might be perceived by a prospective employer as a job-hopper. Or maybe you had to take time off to care for a family member and have an employment gap. Do not ignore these challenges; rather, address them on your résumé. If you're not sure how to do this, seek advice. If potential red flags appear on your résumé and you don't address them, chances are you won't get asked in for an interview.

- *Guideline #10: Don't confuse your audience.* The résumé must *flow*. You want to build excitement and positive momentum while prospective employers read through your résumé. You don't want hiring authorities to suddenly stop reading your résumé because they are confused. You don't want the readers to lose positive momentum by confounding them with overlapping jobs, conflicting job titles, or a disorganized format. Your résumé should be easy to read, easy to follow, and easy to understand.

- *Guideline #11: Embellish at your own risk.* In troubled economic times and during periods of high unemployment, many job seekers will embellish or outright lie on their résumés to secure employment. Employers are well aware of this. Many companies will terminate the interview or your employment if they discover you lied on your résumé. Yes, you have to be resourceful and aggressive to get your foot in the door. But keep in mind that today employers are conducting extensive background and reference checks more than ever before. If you lie on your résumé to get your foot in the door, chances are when they find out, you'll get the boot.

- *Guideline #12: Hire a professional.* Remember the definition of a job seeker I posted at the front of this book? Take a moment and go back to the definition, and study all the aspects of the job campaign you have to master or be proficient in. CEOs of Fortune 500 companies would be hard-pressed to master or be proficient in that many disciplines. They have finance professionals, sales teams, IT departments, management personnel, and consultants to help them. However, most job seekers conduct the job campaign solely on their own.

The process of designing and conducting a job transition campaign is a complex and, oftentimes, overwhelming one that requires a team effort. Indeed, writing résumés and securing a new job are sales and marketing activities. The majority of job seekers are uncomfortable with or downright fearful of selling themselves. Most successful companies hire advertising agencies and marketing firms to market their products and services. This is because advertising agencies are expert at marketing. Athletes and entertainers have agents to promote their value to optimize their compensation. Who do you have working for you? You, most likely, are not an expert at marketing yourself. You haven't been conditioned or trained to blow your own horn. On the contrary, you've been conditioned not to. You are surely skilled at your vocation or profession, but you're probably not skilled at selling yourself. If you are unable to create a résumé that turns you on and that will turn on a prospective employer, you may want to consider hiring a certified résumé professional who can.

THE FOUR QUESTIONS THAT VALUE-BASED RÉSUMÉS MUST ANSWER

Your résumé must answer four critical questions, and the first three questions must be answered in 15 to 20 seconds. The four questions are:

1. What position(s) are you seeking or what are you qualified to do that would be of value to our company or organization?
2. What results and contributions make you better than other qualified candidates?
3. What skills, qualifications, and assets do you bring to the job that would lead us to believe you can produce the results you say you can produce?
4. Can you provide specific results (achievements) that you produced in the past that would indicate that you can produce them in the future?

THE LAW OF MESSAGING

The *Law of Messaging* states that for most jobs, *there are about six to eight messages that you have to communicate that will make 90 percent of the difference between getting an interview and not getting an interview and between getting a job offer and being a runner-up.* Said differently, there are only about six to eight things that determine 90 percent of your value to a prospective employer. Consider, if you will, the U.S. presidential election process. There are only a handful of issues (about six to eight) that all candidates run on to win the presidency of the United States. Whichever candidate makes the best case in addressing those few issues will win. The same holds true for most jobs. When you identify those six to eight messages that will make the most difference in getting an interview and in winning a job offer, you'll design your résumé (and your job transition campaign) around those messages to give yourself a significant advantage over your competition. The messages must collectively answer the questions, "Why should I hire you?" and "What makes you the best qualified candidate for the job?"

There are three types of messages that will be used to create the showcase or headline you will create at the top of your résumé. It is in the showcase where you will send your powerful 15-to–20-second message communicating that you are a highly qualified job candidate! The three types of message are:

1. The *Ultimate Results* messages
2. The *Core Strengths* messages
3. The *Value-Added* messages

1. The Ultimate Results Messages

The Ultimate Results messages are the most important messages you can communicate because *they are the single most essential messages prospective employers want to see on your résumé.* Again, it's all about what you can do for them! The Ultimate Results messages communicate to prospective companies and hiring authorities your value, your worth to them—in other words, what you get paid to produce.

An effective way to determine the Ultimate Results messages is to answer the following questions: If you were to be hired today, what specific performance standards will you be measured on at your first annual review—a year from now? You get paid for producing results, so what results will you produce that will indicate to a company that you are the best candidate for the job? When you answer these questions, you'll have your Ultimate Results messages. What follows are examples of the Ultimate Results messages for five different jobs (I will use the same five jobs illustrating all three messages).

A Teacher

- To significantly enhance the educational experience leading to an enriched and rewarding life for all students

A Sales Professional

- To significantly increase sales, expand market share, and provide unparalleled levels of customer service to contribute to organizational growth and profit objectives

An IT College Graduate

- To advance the goals and objectives of the IT department by utilizing strong programming skills and to improve organizational efficiencies and productivity through the use of state-of-the-art technologies

A Return-to-Work Candidate

- To utilize skills and abilities to meet organizational goals in a loyal, dependable, and professional manner

A CEO

- To increase global presence, product mix, and market share to improve and maintain shareholder earnings and value

When you correctly identify the Ultimate Results messages, you have identified the main reason a company or organization would hire you. Not only will this STAND OUT on your résumé, but it will also make you a more confident and effective interviewee.

2. The Core Strengths Messages

Once you have identified your Ultimate Results messages, you have only to *determine your six to eight core strengths that would lead a hiring manager or prospective employer to believe you can produce the Ultimate Results*. Core strengths would include skills, qualifications, and talents you have that make you valuable and that are *the most important criteria for the job as perceived by the prospective employer.* The Core Strengths messages are messages that communicate those specific skills and qualifications that you will use in your day-to-day activities to produce results and meet or exceed company performance standards.

An effective method for identifying these qualities is to pretend you are writing a book entitled *The Six to Eight Skills You Must Master and Qualifications You Must Have to Become an EXTRAORDINARY* (insert your particular job title, profession, or vocation here). What would those six to eight skills and qualifications be? Imagine you'll write an entire chapter for each skill and qualification to ensure readers of your book that they are mastering the *right* skills and attaining the *right* knowledge and qualifications to be EXTRAORDINARY at their jobs.

Be careful not to be too general or overly fluffy when identifying your Core Strengths messages. It's fine for graduating students or return-to-work candidates to say they have good organizational and communication skills, are loyal and dependable, are "people" persons, and are results oriented. However, these would not be valuable messages for a senior executive because these messages are way too general and fluffy for this level job. Core Strengths messages for senior-level executives might include being highly skilled in mergers and acquisitions, identifying and capitalizing on new and existing market opportunities, turning around underperforming and troubled operations, and utilizing knowledge gained in an MBA program to develop best practices to optimize efficiency and ensure bottom-line performance.

The following are eight Core Strengths messages for each of the five sample professions I noted previously. They follow the Ultimate Results messages.

A Teacher

- To significantly enhance the educational experience leading to an enriched and rewarding life for all students
  1. Improve reading and writing skills
  2. Establish classroom management and discipline
  3. Integrate real-life experiences into the classroom
  4. Introduce real-life experiences outside the classroom
  5. Serve as an effective student-parent liaison
  6. Work collaboratively with administration and peers
  7. Possess strong academic credentials
  8. Have nine years of experience supported by excellent references

A Sales Professional

- To significantly increase sales, expand market share, and provide unparalleled levels of customer service to contribute to organizational growth and profit objectives
  1. Perform in-depth market analysis and create growth plans
  2. Lead generation, networking, and relationship building
  3. Demonstrate high-impact presentation and closing skills
  4. Assess client needs, and effectively overcome objections to sale
  5. Establish new territories and turn around underperforming ones
  6. Initiate new product/service launch
  7. Identify and capitalize on new and existing business opportunities
  8. Provide groundbreaking levels of customer service

An IT College Graduate

- To advance the goals and objectives of the IT department by utilizing strong programming skills and to improve organizational efficiencies and productivity through the use of state-of-the-art technologies

    1. Perl, MySQL, Linux, Apache, Mason, XML, XSL, HTML, JavaScript, Java, MS C11, ASP, 8086 Assembly, Fortran, COBOL, network firewall and hack-proof server installation and configuration, and automatic mass Web site building

    2. Internet-based public relations for online applications

    3. Network administration

    4. Wireless applications

    5. Speech recognition

    6. Excellent customer service skills

    7. Complex, technical troubleshooting and problem solving abilities

    8. Projects on time and within budget

A Return-to-Work Candidate

- To utilize skills and abilities to meet organizational goals in a loyal, dependable, and professional manner

    1. Excellent phone skills

    2. Good communication skills

    3. Sound judgment, good decision making skills

    4. Good character: honest, trustworthy, dependable

    5. Assignments completed on time

    6. Willingness to go the extra mile

    7. Team player

    8. High school graduate

A CEO

- To increase global presence, product mix, and market share to improve and maintain shareholder earnings and value

  1. Mergers and acquisitions
  2. Reengineering and change management
  3. International corporate leadership experience
  4. Visionary strategist; identify and pursue new growth opportunities
  5. Board member and shareholder relations management
  6. Developer of world-class teams to achieve world-class results
  7. MBA from Oxford in international business
  8. Skilled in raising capital for growth and expansion

3. The Value-Added Messages

Value-Added messages communicate added value that you bring to the job that goes beyond the call of duty. In other words, *Value-Added messages communicate to potential hiring managers and prospective employers not only that you have the skills and qualifications to do the job better than other qualified candidates, but that you bring more to the job than what's required.* This added value can be the difference between a job offer and a rejection letter. In many cases, Value-Added messages are the critical messages that differentiate you from your competition. I often refer to this as the *differential factor.*

For example, suppose you are seeking a job as a retail manager. You might bring added value by *being fluent in English, Spanish, and French.* Being trilingual may *not* be part of the job description but can be a valuable asset when working with diverse employees and customers who speak Spanish and French. This Value-Added message may tip the scale in your favor. Possibly you are seeking a job as a fifth grade teacher. If you are an expert in computers and computer programming, these skills may not be part of the job description but might be perceived as having high value to an academic institution. If you are an expert electrician, but you are also highly skilled in sales, this added value of contributing to new business development efforts might be the differentiator, the added skill that will help you land a job quickly in tough markets.

When you combine the Value-Added messages with the Ultimate Results and Core Strengths messages, you will have all the messages you need to conduct a flawless job transition campaign and to create the showcase for your résumé.

A Teacher

- To significantly enhance the educational experience leading to an enriched and rewarding life for all students

  1. Improve reading and writing skills
  2. Establish classroom management and discipline
  3. Integrate real-life experiences into the classroom
  4. Introduce real-life experiences outside the classroom
  5. Serve as an effective student-parent liaison
  6. Work collaboratively with administration and peers
  7. Possess strong academic credentials
  8. Have nine years of experience supported by excellent references

- *Value-Added message:* Have a master's degree in library science *(Able to assist and contribute to library and media services)*

A Sales Professional

- To significantly increase sales, expand market share, and provide unparalleled levels of customer service to contribute to organizational growth and profit objectives

  1. Perform in-depth market analysis and create growth plans
  2. Lead generation, networking, and relationship building
  3. Demonstrate high-impact presentation and closing skills
  4. Assess client needs, and effectively overcome objections to sale
  5. Establish new territories and turn around underperforming ones

6. Initiate new product/service launch

7. Identify and capitalize on new and existing business opportunities

8. Provide groundbreaking levels of customer service

- *Value-Added message:* Have an existing book of business *(Able to deliver immediate sales and growth opportunities)*

An IT College Graduate

- To advance the goals and objectives of the IT department by utilizing strong programming skills and to improve organizational efficiencies and productivity through the use of state-of-the-art technologies

  1. Perl, MySQL, Linux, Apache, Mason, XML, XSL, HTML, JavaScript, Java, MS C11, ASP, 8086 Assembly, Fortran, COBOL, network firewall and hack-proof server installation and configuration, and automatic mass Web site building

  2. Internet-based public relations for online applications

  3. Network administration

  4. Wireless applications

  5. Speech recognition

  6. Excellent customer service skills

  7. Complex, technical troubleshooting and problem solving abilities

  8. Complete projects on time and within budget

- *Value-Added message:* Have my Dale Carnegie Public Speaking Certification *(Able to professionally train and present new technologies and services effectively to employees and customers)*

A Return-to-Work Candidate

- To utilize skills and abilities to meet organizational goals in a loyal, dependable, and professional manner

  1. Excellent phone skills

2. Good communication skills

3. Sound judgment, good decision making skills

4. Good character: honest, trustworthy, and dependable

5. Assignments completed on time

6. Willingness to go the extra mile

7. Team player

8. High school graduate

- *Value-Added message:* Have own transportation and able to work a flexible work schedule *(Provides a great degree of dependability and flexibility compared with others who may be dependent on the bus or others unable to work a flexible work schedule)*

A CEO

- To increase global presence, product mix, and market share to improve and maintain shareholder earnings and value

  1. Mergers and acquisitions

  2. Reengineering and change management

  3. International corporate leadership experience

  4. Visionary strategist; identify and pursue new growth opportunities

  5. Board member and shareholder relations management

  6. Developer of world-class teams to achieve world-class results

  7. Possess an MBA from Oxford in international business

  8. Skilled in raising capital for growth and expansion

- *Value-Added message:* Have built and managed two million-dollar companies *(Able to build a third one)*

Once you have identified your Ultimate Results, Core Strengths, and Value-Added messages, you have an exceptionally solid foundation upon which you can design the showcase of your résumé. You will have the critical messages that will engage the reader and create excitement in 15 to 20 seconds.

Later, when you work on the employment and education section, along with the other sections, of your résumé, you will know exactly what job responsibilities and achievements and what educational highlights and internship experiences to emphasize that will provide clear and concise evidence that you can use your skills and qualifications competently and produce significant results!

THE SHOWCASE FORMAT

The showcase format is a résumé presentation that communicates your Ultimate Results, Core Strengths, and Value-Added messages in 15 to 20 seconds professionally and in a reader-friendly manner. The showcase engages the reader and builds initial excitement in you as a viable job candidate. Pick up any newspaper or magazine, and study the advertisements. In most cases, you'll notice a headline or see a picture with an accompanying headline. Effective marketing strategically positions information and pictures to capture the prospective buyer's attention quickly and with strong emotion. When you create your résumé, you'll want to insert a headline atop the document as well.

When you review the sample résumés on the following pages, you'll notice that the three messages, the Ultimate Results, Core Strengths, and Value-Added messages, make up most of the showcase. Remember that your résumé must answer three questions in 15 to 20 seconds: 1) *What position(s) are you seeking or what are you qualified to do that would be of value to our company or organization?* 2) *What results and contributions make you better than other qualified candidates?* and 3) *What skills, qualifications, and assets do you bring to the job that would lead us to believe you can produce the results you say you can produce?* Your showcase is designed to answer those three questions in that time frame. What follows are examples of showcases for a teacher and a sales professional.

Showcase for a Teacher

STEPHANIE SANDS

6868 South Flagler Drive • West Palm Beach, FL 33401

(561) 555–8787 • email@email.com

Seeking position as…

Teacher / Educator
Combining Outstanding Technology, Leadership, and Teaching Experience
Master's Degree in Library Science

*Strong desire to enhance the educational experience for
all students leading to enriched and rewarding lives*

PERSONAL INTRODUCTION

A seasoned professional with a passion for combining business experience and educational qualifications to make a significant contribution in the field of education.

Core Professional Strengths:

- Energetic presentation/teaching skills
- Maintain classroom discipline
- Work well with culturally diverse populations
- Meet individual/group needs
- Extracurricular participation
- Work well with superiors and peers
- Facilitate established curriculum
- IT/technology
- Real-life integration
- Problem/conflict resolution
- Effective student-parent liaison
- Professional/highly ethical

Showcase for a Sales Professional

Hector Gonzalez
21009 North Shore Avenue • Winnetka, IL 60093
(847) 555–9119 • email@email.com

SENIOR-LEVEL NEW BUSINESS DEVELOPMENT EXECUTIVE
Significantly Increase Sales / Expand Market Share
Outmaneuver Major Competitors to Establish Market Dominance

- 25 years of success in favorable and recessionary global economies
- Lead generation, networking, and relationship building
- Perform in-depth market analysis; create strategic/ growth plans
- Identify and capitalize on new and existing marketing opportunities
- Territorial start-up, turnaround, and growth management
- Build and nurture key strategic relationships and partnerships
- Key account management and retention; ensure unparalleled levels of service

Have existing book of business to increase sales immediately

Senior-Level Sales Executive with a reputation for providing unparalleled levels of customer service and contributing to organizational growth and profit objectives.

THE TWO COMPONENTS OF THE EMPLOYMENT SECTION

Once you have developed a powerful showcase, you are ready to answer the fourth question that your résumé must address: *can you provide specific results (achievements) that you produced in the past that would indicate that you can produce them in the future?* In most cases, the employment section will answer this final question. However, if you are a graduating student or one who has little or no direct work experience, your internships, academic highlights, and extracurricular activities, including volunteer work and community service, will be emphasized.

When you work on the employment section, you'll want to address two distinct components for each job or position that will appear on the résumé: 1) your detailed job responsibilities or job description and 2) your achievements and contributions, the results you produced. How you accomplish this is up to you. What follows are two samples of how most hiring professionals, human resource managers, and executive recruiters like to view the employment section.

Preferred Presentation
(Job Description PLUS Bulleted Achievements)

GREAT SCOTT UNIFORM COMPANY, Boston, MA   2000 to Current
General Sales & Operations Manager

Directed the successful start-up of a niche market law enforcement uniform company specializing in private security and in-house security organizations. Company generates $3.6 million in annual revenues serving clients nationwide. Divide time equally between sales and operations. Presently supervise 19 employees including warehouse manager, alterations manager, sales coordinator, and office manager. Fully responsible for a 9,000 sq. ft. location including a 6,000 sq. ft. warehouse with $350k in inventory. Coordinate proactive safety and security protocols. Establish key benchmarks to optimize efficiency and productivity. Develop/manage a $1.7 million annual operating budget, coordinate purchasing and vendor relations, and ensure high customer service standards for more than 190 national accounts. Full charge P&L responsibility.

Specific Accomplishments

- Grew start-up operation to an industry leader generating $3.6 million in annual sales.
- Developed company "brand label" (*Great Scott*) that improved market share 18%.
- Private labeling efforts increased sales 47% and boosted gross profit margins 11%.
- Achieved 16% net profits—some 7% above national industry average.
- Spearheaded Just-In-Time inventory process that reduced inventory 21%.
- Identified 3 profitable acquisitions that added $600,000 in yearly sales.
- Closed 4 national accounts (IBM, Wackenhut, Pinkerton, and Raytheon).
- Awarded "Distributor of the Year" by *Made to Measure Magazine*.
- Awarded "Quality Dealer" award by *Made to Measure Magazine* 7 consecutive years.
- Positioned company for successful, profitable sale, with 1-year working contract.

NEXT BEST PRESENTATION
(Job Description and Achievements Combined in a Bulleted Format)

GREAT SCOTT UNIFORM CO., Boston, MA   2000 to Current
General Sales & Operations Manager

- Directed the successful start-up of a niche market law enforcement uniform company.
- Manage $3.6 million operation with a $1.7 million annual budget.
- Divide time equally between sales and operations. Presently supervise 19 employees.
- Manage a 9,000 sq. ft. location including a 6,000 sq. ft. warehouse ($350k in inventory).
- Grew start-up operation to an industry leader generating $3.6 million in annual sales.
- Developed company "brand label" (*Great Scott*) that improved market share 18%.
- Private labeling efforts increased sales 47% and boosted gross profit margins 11%.
- Achieved 16% net profits—some 7% above national industry average.
- Spearheaded Just-In-Time inventory process that reduced inventory 21%.
- Identified 3 profitable acquisitions that added $600,000 in yearly sales.
- Closed 4 national accounts (IBM, Wackenhut, Pinkerton, and Raytheon).
- Awarded "Distributor of the Year" by *Made to Measure Magazine*.
- Awarded "Quality Dealer" award by *Made to Measure Magazine* 7 consecutive years.
- Positioned company for successful, profitable sale, with 1-year working contract.

PERSONAL INFORMATION

Unless there is a strategic reason to include it, I suggest you leave off personal information including age, place of birth, marital status, and other nonrelevant information. *Remember, though, there are no rules.* If you have a legitimate reason for including personal information, do so. For instance, when you prepare a federal résumé for federal jobs, you will, in most cases, be asked to supply federal job compliance information including your social security number, proof of citizenship, and date of birth. If you are seeking a job as a physical education teacher, you may want to include sports you are involved in. Once again, think strategically. Put yourself in the shoes of a hiring manager who will be reading your résumé, and ask yourself, "If I did not know this person (meaning you), would the personal information be at all relevant or important to the hiring process?" If so, leave it in. If not, leave it off.

RELIGIOUS AND POLITICAL ISSUES

I will provide a very short and obvious statement regarding religion and politics as they relate to your résumé. I advise you to leave all information relating to religious, political, and other possibly *controversial activities and subjects* off the résumé unless you have a strategic reason to include it.

SALARY AND SALARY HISTORY ON RÉSUMÉS

As a rule, salary history is not included on résumés. At the risk of being redundant, if you are seeking a federal job, you may need to include prior pay grades and salaries on your document. But the general guideline is that unless you have a well-thought-out reason for doing so, omit salary from your résumé.

REASONS FOR LEAVING PRIOR EMPLOYMENT

Traditionalists will argue that you never include *reasons for leaving* on your résumé. However, times have changed. If you have had many jobs in a short period of time, which might cause you to be perceived as an unreliable job candidate, you may want to provide short, effective, and nondefensive reasons for leaving prior positions. If you had to leave a job to care for an ill parent, this might also be a time when you would include a reason for leaving. The important thing to remember is that *you want to include reasons for leaving if they enhance your ability to better communicate with hiring authorities for the purpose of neutralizing or eliminating influences that could be perceived as negative. Caution:* There is a fine line between providing understandable *reasons for leaving* and coming across as overly defensive. The reasons must be well thought out, brief, and strategically sound.

GIMMICKS AND OMISSIONS

What is a gimmick to one person may be a foot in the door for another. Marketing and self-promotion are about capturing the emotions of a prospect; they're about enticing a prospective employer to get excited about you and your ability to fill an employment vacancy. I have successfully used pictures, graphs, color, cartoons, testimonials, graphics, and other nontraditional strategies to help thousands of people land great jobs at great pay, at all levels! *Years ago a well-respected executive recruiter from Boston told me that if a candidate is going to err, err on the side of ingenuity and creativity, not boredom. She told me that at least the creative résumé will get read; the boring one won't ever see the light of day.* So here's the best advice I can offer. Create a professionally exciting document! I would argue that gimmicks don't work. But creativity and originality presented in a professional manner will STAND OUT and get noticed.

One last important point I must make here. People who read résumés and hire employees are *not* stupid! If you include dates in your employment section but leave them off in your education section because you don't want to show your age, you did! They know all the tricks! Be tactical in your approach, don't underestimate the intelligence of hiring and employment professionals, and don't come across as devious or deceptive.

EDUCATION AND TRAINING EXPERIENCE

If you have a master's degree, you do not have to include your high school education. Include the highest degrees you have, but use common sense; you don't have to go back to middle school. In addition to formal education, employers want to know what you do to continually expand your knowledge and improve your professional skills. Indeed, change takes place at lightning speed these days, and employers want to know you are keeping up with the speed of change. What continuing education courses have you attended? How many personal development seminars have you completed? How many professional improvement workshops have you attended? What computer skills are you proficient in? Here's something to keep in mind: *if you go to bed at night the same as you awoke in the morning, you'll be worth less (or worthless?) to the marketplace tomorrow.* Be sure to practice personal development, and include this important information on your résumé in addition to your formal education. Additionally, unless you have strategic reasons to place them elsewhere, your education section is a good place to include all pertinent licenses and certifications and any other credentialing you might have earned.

Where you place the education section within the résumé is up to you. If your education is about the same as that of your competition, it probably should appear after the employment section. On the other hand, if your education can be positioned on your résumé as a unique "selling point" and may be more impressive than that of most of your competition, you might want to put the education section before the experience section. If you are a recent graduate, you may also want to position the education section before the experience section. Internships can go in the education section or in the employment section or have their own section. You determine how you want the reader of your résumé to read the résumé.

MILITARY EXPERIENCE

If you have military experience, thank you for serving your country. Three hundred million-plus Americans are indebted to you. Your service is held in high esteem by a grateful nation. *So I urge you to present your military information on your résumé as proudly as you wore the uniform.* However, include only relevant information that would interest prospective employers. For instance, if you served 25 years ago, you need only list the branch of the service you were in, title, rank, possibly where you served, honorable discharge, and dates of service. If you spent the past three years in the armed services maintaining and repairing vehicles and are seeking a civilian job repairing automobiles, you will treat your military section the same as you would the employment section, noting both your specific responsibilities and your key achievements, awards, and contributions. Include only information that is directly or indirectly relevant to your next job.

RELEVANT ACTIVITIES AND PROFESSIONAL AFFILIATIONS

If you have space on your résumé and want to include relevant activities and professional affiliations, include them. If you are a member of professional associations, trade organizations, and business groups, include them. If you have volunteered or are active in community service projects, include them. If you play golf and, in your line of work, deals are consummated on the golf course, include this. On the other hand, if you are seeking a position as a bookkeeper and you like to travel and enjoy gardening, unless you are looking to become a traveling bookkeeper or are trying to land a bookkeeping job with a landscaping company, it might be best if you leave this off the résumé. Use common sense, and include only information that hiring authorities will find valuable in making a favorable hiring decision.

DON'T CONDUCT THE INTERVIEW IN THE RÉSUMÉ

Here's a good analogy. Your résumé is like a book report. You don't tell the whole story in a book report; you simply provide a synopsis of the key highlights that STAND OUT as the most important information taken from the book. The same is true when writing a résumé. Your résumé must dangle the carrot, but not tell the whole story. Your résumé must communicate your value and enthusiastically engage the reader, not provide a long-winded, never-ending biography of your professional life. Your résumé must provide highlights of your professional experience that STAND OUT as the most important information that prospective employers would find valuable. Do not tell the whole story; don't conduct the interview in the résumé.

COVER LETTERS

Most people today, including hiring authorities, are living a high-stress life. They are being bombarded by e-mail, voice mail, U.S. mail, and junk mail. They take calls from cell phones, business phones, and home phones, not to mention the demands for attention from many other voices. *Most HR managers, executive recruiters, and hiring managers are placing less and less importance on cover letters. Yes, they are still a part of the process, but they play a less significant role.* The reason for this is simple: information overload and too little time to read. If your résumé is strong and effective, the cover letter becomes a very short, formal introduction to your résumé. Here are eight tips for writing effective cover letters.

1. Address the cover letter to a specific person, ensuring the correct name, title, company, and address. This shows respect for the person you are sending the résumé to.

2. "To Whom It May Concern" salutations should be used *only* if you can't determine the name of the hiring person or the company (for instance, when responding to a blind ad).

3. If you were referred by someone, be sure this is included in the first sentence of the cover letter: "Jennifer Wells suggested I contact you in regard to an accounts receivable position you have open …" It's an attention grabber.

4. If asked to include salary history or requirements, you must address this or risk being disqualified. Provide a healthy range, such as "Over the past five years I have earned between $35,000 and $48,000. However, I am open to any reasonable offer consistent with my ability to produce results and meet your performance expectations." If asked for

salary requirements, use the same strategy: "I am aware that the salary range for a loss prevention manager in the Houston area averages between $75,000 and $110,000. Given my experience and, most importantly, my ability to make significant contributions to your company, I would hope to be on the upper end of this scale."

5. If you are sending the résumé out electronically, the cover letter can be inserted as the e-mail itself; just attach your résumé. If you prefer that your cover letter is the first page of the attachment, that's fine. But the general guideline is not to attach multiple files. Make it easy on the hiring manager and send only one attachment or file to open (unless you have a good reason to do otherwise).

6. Do not rehash what is on the résumé. This is disrespectful of the reader's time. If you have done a good job with your résumé, you want the cover letter to quickly entice the hiring manager to read your résumé.

7. Cover letters should not be preachy. Sales managers know that sales are the heartbeat of any company; you don't have to lecture them on this. Nurse supervisors know the importance of compassionate patient care; you don't have to tell them what they already know. Keep the letter short and concise. The cover letter is not the place to preach or teach. It's the place to invite recipients to read your résumé!

8. Finally, the four most important words on the cover letter are *"I respect your time."* The following cover letter is a sample template to use in these challenging and troubled times. Notice the first four words of the second paragraph.

ROBERT SMITH

200 Main Street• Hollywood, FL 33021
(954) 555–2345• email@email.com

May 24, 20__

Mrs. Patrice Wellington, Assistant Manager
Beachwear International
3232 Ocean Boulevard, Suite 300
North Miami Beach, FL 33089

Dear Mrs. Wellington:

I am interested in applying for the position with Beachwear International as Purchasing Manager and have enclosed my résumé for your review. I am certain that I can be a valuable asset to your team and meet and exceed the goals and objectives for this position.

I respect your time and feel confident that my value, past achievements, and ability to contribute are well outlined in my résumé. If you feel, as I do, that I would be a significant member of your professional staff, I would welcome an interview at your earliest convenience.

Thank you for your consideration, and I look forward to hearing back from you.

Sincerely,

Robert Smith
Encl: Résumé

A CASE FOR MULTIPLE RÉSUMÉS

If you have multiple job objectives, you will probably need multiple résumés for each objective. The competition for jobs today is intense. Many job seekers are creating individual résumés for each job they are applying for, knowing that each résumé must communicate precise messages that are critical to getting an interview. The skills sets, qualifications, and value messages are different for a sales associate than a sales manager. The skills sets, qualifications, and value messages are different for a manager seeking an executive-level position than a mid-level position. And if you are considering a job as either a social worker or a customer service representative, you'll need two completely different résumés because the skills sets, qualifications, and value messages are completely different. Landing a job in troubled times requires an innovative and dedicated effort to distinguish yourself from the massive competition you're facing. *In troubled economies and during times of high unemployment, you must work smarter and more intelligently than ever before. This means you'll probably need to develop multiple versions of your résumé to precisely align your skills and qualifications with the specific requirements of each job for which you are applying.* When it comes to landing a job during tough times, don't be lazy! Create multiple résumés because your competition probably won't. Undoubtedly, this gives you the advantage!

THE REFERENCE PORTFOLIO— *THE SECRET WEAPON OF THE JOB TRANSITION CAMPAIGN*

The reference portfolio is a powerful tool that deviates from traditional ways of thinking. But the truth is, the reference portfolio may be the most powerful tool you'll have in your job transition arsenal. But before we go any further, stop and grab a few books from your library shelves. Look on the back covers of the books. Chances are, you'll see a number of testimonials, most of which are only two or three sentences in length. But each testimonial *sings the praise* of the book and entices potential readers to want to read the book. A reference portfolio is exactly the same. A reference portfolio is a one-page document with four to six testimonials that will *sing your praises* and entice hiring professionals to want to meet and hire you!

In troubled economies and during times of high unemployment, many job candidates will embellish, exaggerate, and outright lie on their résumés. Hiring managers, human resource professionals, and executive recruiters are well aware of this. In fact, they expect it! In favorable economies with low unemployment, most hiring authorities read résumés with a healthy skepticism anyway. But in tough economic times, where many people are in *survival mode*, hiring authorities read résumés with a great deal of skepticism. A reference portfolio is an effective tool to eliminate the negative manner in which most hiring professionals will read your résumé!

The portfolio is made up of professional references that will confirm and validate that the achievements and contributions you noted on your résumé are truthful and accurate. If you are a student or a recent college graduate or if you are returning to the workforce or have limited professional references, you'll want to identify those references, professional and personal, who will attest to the fact that you are a valuable and viable candidate able to produce results and contribute to organizational goals. *Once you have identified and confirmed that four to six people agree to endorse you, I advise you to write the reference statements yourself!* Athletes and celebrities do not write the advertisements for the products and services they endorse. And your "endorsers" should not write the advertisements for you, either! I suggest you write the testimonial and then send it to your references so they can review the statement and make whatever edits they may want to make. Once the reference is complete, they should keep a copy in their files so when a prospective employer calls them to validate their reference about you, they can easily refer to it.

Once you have your reference portfolio, I suggest you send it along with your cover letter and résumé. If you are e-mailing your résumé, the reference portfolio should be the last page. Again, you want to attach only one file to an e-mail. One of the many advantages to having a reference portfolio is that you don't need to have numerous reference letters on company letterhead, which is fortunate as most companies are unwilling to provide them anyway. If you have a boss that will give you a reference but can't do it on company letterhead or on company time, he or she may be willing to do so via a personal e-mail address from home.

Finally, once you have a reference portfolio, you can add the following P.S. and insert it at the bottom of your cover letter. **And I suggest you bold it** so the P.S. is a focal point of the cover letter. By doing this, the hiring professionals reading your résumé will do so with confidence that what they are reading is, indeed, accurate and truthful.

PS: I have included my reference portfolio to assure you that the information and achievements contained on my résumé are truthful and accurate.

A Sample Reference Portfolio

JUSTIN T. WINTERS
1750 Greystone Court • Lansing, MI 48912
(754) 555.3232• Cell: (754) 555.1212
email@email.com

REFERENCE PORTFOLIO

John P. Hendricks, Director of Operations   email@email.com
THE MIDWEST GOLF COMPANIES

"Justin Winters was the best assistant warehouse manager The MGC has ever had. He single-handedly designed and implemented a JIT inventory program that reduced inventory 23% while improving customer services levels to a record 98.7%. He is well respected by the 13 employees who report to him, and he always motivates highly productive teams."

Ed Shuman, Senior Buyer   **(212.555.6012)**
PING CORPORATION

"Justin Winters is the ultimate warehouse management professional. As assistant manager for The Midwest Golf Companies, we worked exclusively with him and developed a positive and effective win-win relationship. He negotiated a number of innovative terms and conditions with our company that reduced his organization's on-hand inventory levels 25% but increased annual sales volume with our company 15%. Justin's innovative program was so successful, we are now offering it to our customers nationwide. He is creative, resourceful, and relentless in meeting his company's growth and bottom-line objectives, and firm but fair in his relations with vendors."

Susan B. Johnston, Assistant Warehouse Manager   (561.555.7279)
SOUTH MICHIGAN GOLF OUTLET

"I would not have the job I have today without the training, supervision, and inspiration of Justin Winters. I worked for Justin when I worked for Midwest Golf for six years. During that time, he taught me how to be a highly effective leader in warehouse management. So few people ever get the opportunity to learn from a true professional and an authentic human being. I can't imagine anyone more qualified than Justin to be a warehouse manager in a high-volume, growth-driven environment."

Frank Fordum, Warehouse Manager   email@email.com
THE MIDWEST GOLF COMPANIES

"Justin Winters has worked as my assistant warehouse manager for the past nine years. There is not one aspect of high-volume warehouse operations that he is not proficient at. In fact, it is said that everyone is replaceable— but when Justin left our company, it left a void I am not sure can be filled, not only because of his extraordinary skills, but also because of the intangible attributes he brings to the job—like a smile on his face and a positive attitude every day. He is sorely missed."

FIVE SAMPLE RÉSUMÉS

Five sample résumés follow. Please pay particular attention to how the showcases for each discipline include the Ultimate Results, Core Strengths, and Value-Added messages discussed earlier in this chapter and are nicely integrated at the top of each résumé.

STEPHANIE SANDS

6868 South Flagler Drive • West Palm Beach, FL 33401
(561) 555–8787• email@email.com

Teacher / Educator

9 years Outstanding Experience
Master's Degree in Library Science

**"Enhance the educational experience for all students
leading to enriched lives"**

Introduction

A seasoned business professional with a passion for combining business experience and education to make a significant contribution in the field of education. Recognized for collaborative approach in meeting quality standards and organizational missions and facilitating positive change.

Core Professional Strengths:

- Improve reading and writing skills; classroom management and discipline
- Integrate real-life experiences into and outside the classroom
- Introduce effective computer/IT technologies to enhance the learning experience
- Act as an effective student-parent liaison; work collaboratively with administration and peers

FORMAL EDUCATION

Master's in Library Science, 1999   Florida Atlantic University, Boca Raton, FL
Bachelor's in Education, 1996   University of Miami, Coral Gables, FL

- Board Certified, American Board for Certification of Teacher Excellence

PROFESSIONAL EXPERIENCE

PALM BEACH COUNTY SCHOOL DISTRICT, West Palm Beach, FL   2001 to Current
Lower School Teacher
Responsible for all aspects of education at the lower school level with emphasis on math, English, science, social studies, and history. Ensure a positive learning classroom environment and work collaboratively with administration, peers, students, and parents to meet a broad range of objectives.

- Disney World Teacher Award (top 100 out of 5,000 teachers)
- Teacher of the Year finalist, 2008
- Recipient of Teacher of Excellence award, 2007
- More than 30 performance awards over past 7 years
- Nominated for WPEC News 12 Educator of Excellence award
- Delegate to National Teacher's Convention, Washington, DC, 2004–current
- Assisted more than 40 students to gain admission to the prestigious School of the Arts

EXPERIENCE PRIOR TO 2001

Middle School Teacher   Jupiter Elementary, Jupiter, FL
Lower School Teacher   The Benjamin School, Palm Beach, FL

RELEVANT ACTIVITIES

National Teachers Educational Association   Palm Beach County/National
Florida Society for Academic Excellence   Tallahassee, FL
Music Teacher/Assist in Library Services

HECTOR GONZALEZ

21009 North Shore Avenue • Winnetka, IL 60093

(847) 555–9119 • LinkedIn: Hector Gonzales • email@email.com

SENIOR-LEVEL NEW BUSINESS DEVELOPMENT EXECUTIVE
Significantly Increase Sales / Expand Market Share
Outmaneuver Major Competitors to Establish Market Dominance

- 25 years of success in favorable and recessionary global economies
- Lead generation, networking, and relationship building
- Perform in-depth market analysis, and create strategic/growth plans
- Identify and capitalize on new and existing marketing opportunities
- Territorial start-up, turnaround, and growth management; product launch
- Build and nurture key strategic alliances and partnerships
- Key account management/retention; ensure unparalleled levels of service

Have existing book of business to increase sales immediately

Senior-Level Sales Executive with a reputation for providing unparalleled levels of customer service and contributing to organizational growth and profit objectives.

Professional Experience

CORPORATE PACKAGING, INC., Hollywood, FL   1989 to 2010
Senior Sales Executive
Directed all B2B sales and new business development activities in the South Florida market, servicing more than 180 major accounts generating $6.8 million annually. Performed market analysis and strategies to meet organizational sales and profit objectives. Assisted manufacturing and distribution clients in selecting proper packaging products to meet diverse needs. Helped clients with product specifications to produce customizing packaging products.
- Grew new territory with $0 in revenues to $6.8 million.
- Closed key accounts including Ryder, Carnival Cruise Lines, and the Miami Dolphins.
- Prepared specifications and won $8 million bid (over 10 years) with City of N. Miami Beach.
- Worked with corporate development team to design new packaging equipment that is now generating more than $50 million a year in revenue nationally for the company.

OFFICE DEPOT, Deerfield Beach, FL   1985 to 1989
Senior Sales Executive
Managed Broward County sales efforts selling upscale, high-end office equipment with an average ticket price of $6,500 to local businesses. Developed qualified leads, made comprehensive presentations to senior management, and closed key accounts in competitive market. Ensured high-quality service by making sure that products were delivered on time and properly installed. Trained clients in equipment usage.
- Grew new territory from $2.3 million in sales to more than $7 million in less than 4 years.
- Closed key accounts including hotels, hospitals, municipalities, and local businesses.
- Exceeded sales quota and revenue projections each year.

OHIO STATE UNIVERSITY, Columbus, OH   UNITED STATES ARMY
Bachelor of Science: Civil Engineering, 1984   **Commander, Honorable Discharge, 1983**
- Computer Skills: Word, Excel, PowerPoint, Outlook, and Internet Applications

RYAN ROBINSON

9844 Colonia Way • S. Hackensack, NJ 07605

(201) 555–7337 • email@email.com

Entry-Level IT Professional with Strong Academic/Work Experience
Quick learner and performer, with strong working knowledge of
software, hardware, networking, programming, operating systems,
and security applications

A highly creative, technically skilled individual seeking to advance the goals and objectives of the IT department by utilizing strong programming skills. Poised to improve organizational efficiencies and productivity through the use of state-of-the-art technologies.

Core Strengths:
- Ability to diagnose, troubleshoot, and resolve technical problems.
- Exemplary academic record. Graduated with 3.48 GPA.
- Outstanding communication skills (verbal and written); excellent customer service skills.
- Project management—conception through completion including budget and expense control.

Operating Systems: Windows 2000/ME/XP, Mac OS X, Vista

Applications: MS Office 2000/XP (Word, Excel, PowerPoint, Access), Lotus Notes, Norton Utilities, Adobe Photoshop; Perl, MySQL, Linux, Apache, Mason, XML, XSL, HTML, JavaScript, Java, MS C++, ASP, 8086 Assembly, Fortran, COBOL, network firewall and hack-proof server installation and configuration, and automatic mass Web site building; Internet-based public relations for online businesses; Network administration (LAN/WAN, TCP/IP, VPN) and Wireless and Voice.

Valued-Added Contributions: Ability to contribute to growth and new business development

Education

Bachelor of Science: Computer Science, 2010   University of Arizona, Tucson, AZ
- Vice President: University of Arizona IT Club
- Honors Graduate; Member, Pi Beta Alpha Honor Society

Internships:

Allan Research International, Tucson, AZ   Summer 2007, 2008, and 2009
- **Tech Support Intern:** Operated as service point-of-contact for help desk, helping to diagnose, troubleshoot, and resolve up to 11 tickets a day. Assisted in converting from Windows 2000 to XP to Windows Vista for 38 workstations. Provided daily technical support for e-mail, network, connectivity, telecommunications, peripheral equipment, and system maintenance. Set up computers and installed software. Helped transfer help desk requests from e-mail to Web-based system, reducing IT response time by 21%.

Part-Time Work While in College

University of Arizona, Tucson, AZ   2006, 2007, 2008, and 2009
- **Help Desk Technician:** Tutored students in various operating systems and software applications. Served as mentor in computer labs, and provided emergency technical support for early-morning shift. Helped install 19 new Mac computers for busy lab.

Keywords: Entry-level, Systems Administrator, Network Administrator, Technical Help Desk Coordinator, Technician, Systems Support Engineer, Systems Analyst, PC Technician, IT Troubleshooter, Team Player, Project Management, MAC and PC Expertise, Client Relations, Voice Recognition, Programming.

TARA JOHNSTON
123 Main Street • Atlanta, GA 30339
(555) 363–1234

Seeking HOUSEKEEPING POSITION with Hotel or Hospital
Bilingual: English and Spanish

To utilize skills and abilities to meet organizational goals
in a loyal, dependable, and professional manner

A loyal, trustworthy, and dependable individual with own transportation and able to work a flexible work schedule. A lifelong record of hard work, going the extra mile and producing excellent results. A good working knowledge of the equipment, materials, and methods used in custodial work.

Strengths:

- Organized and goal-oriented
- Take the initiative to solve problems
- Interpersonal skills; a "people" person
- Perform tasks well on short notice

- Follow instructions and company policies
- Complete multiple assignments on time
- Able to make good decisions
- Team player; work well with others

Activities 1990 to Current

Over the past 20 years, I have successfully raised four children; one has graduated high school, and the other three are close to graduating high school. Supplemented income by performing domestic and housecleaning chores on a regular basis. Effectively manage schedule to meet customer needs while being a responsible mother.

Over the past 20 years, I have worked for approximately 15 customers. Basic responsibilities include: Ensuring clean homes, following specific instructions based on the needs of each customer, maintaining a detailed list for each customer to be sure all work that needs to be completed is completed to the customer's satisfaction, and priding myself on going the extra mile at all times. Never lost a customer (except when they moved or passed away). Make recommendations to customers when repairs around the home are necessary. Provide weekly lists for all customers that include specific supplies and equipment needed to do the job well. Highly trustworthy, loyal, dependable, and bondable.

Education/Activities

Pooley High School, Atlanta, GA
High School Graduate, 1980
- "School of Life;" Possess Good Common Sense
- Active Member: PTA; Sing in Church Choir

References

Mr. and Mrs. Wilson DeVos (Customer, 8 years)
(555) 987–6543
Mr. and Mrs. David Goldfarb (Customer, 10 years)
(555) 456–2348

Mrs. Wilma Jefferson (Customer, 11 years)
(555) 345–6789
Mr. and Mrs. John Crow (Customer, 6 years)
(555) 912–8348

HAROLD R. CONNORS

7177 Beacon Circle • Boston, MA 01977

(617) 555–3232 • * LinkedIn: Harold Connors

email@email.com

'C' LEVEL OPERATIONS / MANAGEMENT EXECUTIVE
MBA, Oxford University

Increasing Shareholder Value in Publicly Traded and Private Companies
SEC Reporting and Compliance / Start-Up and Turnaround Management

Technology Integration / Business Development and Expansion
P&L Responsibility /Cash Flow Management

EXECUTIVE PROFILE

A market-driven visionary with outstanding qualifications in directing multi-million-dollar operations in global theaters.

AREAS OF EXPERTISE

- Mergers and acquisitions
- Reengineering and change management
- Board member and shareholder relations
- Raising capital for growth and expansion
- International corporate leadership
- Recruiting and developing world-class teams

PROFESSIONAL EXPERIENCE

DRUCKER ENTERPRISES, Waltham, MA   1991 to Current

CEO

Recruited by Board of Directors to direct and grow this biotechnology, orthopaedic reconstructive implants, trauma, sports medicine, and general medical instruments company. Divide time equally between new business development and operations; built one of the most successful medical instruments company in the Northeast, serving many of the nation's top medical facilities and health-care practitioners. Presently direct 29 employees including sales professionals, technicians, medical support staff, warehouse personnel, and office administration.

Fully responsible for a 10,000 sq. ft. location including a 7,000 sq. ft. warehouse with $2 million in inventory. Establish key benchmarks (best practices) to optimize efficiency and production. Develop and manage an $8.9 million annual operating budget, and ensure sales, growth, and profit forecasts are met. Took over company with sales of $1.1 million in 1991 and developed long-term strategic growth plan that resulted in sales of more than $11 million in 2008.

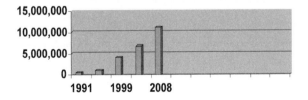

- Increased shareholder earnings to an average of 16% annual ROI.
- Increased market share from 8% to 37%; expected to achieve 50% market share by 2015.
- Recognized in New *England Journal of Medicine* as the Best in Class medical instrument company in New England.

KENNEDY MEDICAL, INC., Detroit, MI   1985 to 1991
VP Sales

Tripled sales volume

Kennedy Medical, a distributor of orthopaedic products with sales of $99k in 1985. Recruited as VP of sales to turn around an unprofitable operation due to poor sales and customer service efforts. Performed in-depth market and competitive analysis and created a five-year growth plan with the goal of tripling sales and reducing expense-to-sales costs by 18%.

- Developed a new market, targeting orthopaedic, neuro- and maxillofacial surgeons; podiatrists; and hospitals. This increased revenues to $2.9 million.
- Created a high-impact direct mail campaign for bone healing stimulators. Distributor sales grew by more than 200% and generated more than $3 million in additional revenues.
- Managed total knee replacement patient outcome and survivorship clinical studies for a highly respected surgeon–clinical investigator. High exposure led to significant new business that ultimately allowed us to hit our target of $21.6 million in annual revenues with a net profit of 11% (some 6% above industry average).

EDUCATION
UNIVERSITY OF MICHIGAN, Ann Arbor, MI
MBA (Emphasis on International Business), 1990 Bachelor of Arts Degree in Economics, 1984
- Certified on OSHA Regulations & Risk Management Protocol for the OR
- Certified Continuing Medical Education Facilitator for Nursing Education by Healthstream
- Graduate of Anthony Robbins' Mastery University Program
- The Dale Carnegie CEO Leadership Seminars (Four-Week Intense Training)
- Member of Toastmasters International
- Board Member for Six Business and Nonprofit Institutions (Details furnished on request)

PROFESSIONAL AFFILIATIONS
Active Member: American Business Association
Active Member: National Orthopaedic Reconstructive Implant Society
Active Member: American Orthotic & Prosthetic Association
Active Member: American Prosthodontic Society, Association
Active Member: The Association for Children's Prosthetic Orthotic Clinics
Active Member: American Orthopaedics Society for Sports Medicine

References and Supporting Documentation Furnished upon Request

A WORD ABOUT BIOS

Bios are normally short, one-page documents providing the bare "essentials" that represent one's value to a targeted audience. They are used primarily by independent contractors, business owners, and entrepreneurs and those who do not feel full-blown résumés are appropriate for their purposes. Bios might appear on a Web site, in a brochure, in a business plan, or as part of a consulting proposal. The following is a sample bio.

Lawrence T. Stanley

4267 Golden Lake Road * Birmingham, MI 48012
(555) 212–9876 * LinkedIn: Lawrence Stanley
www.website.com * email@email.com

SENIOR CONSULTANT
Operations / Logistics / Global Expansion / Process Improvement

Lawrence T. Stanley is a lifelong resident of Birmingham, Michigan, where he lives with his wife, Norma, and his three children, Michael (20), Elena (17), and Derrick (15). Mr. Stanley attended and graduated from the United States Military Academy at West Point prior to entering the United States Army. His military service took him throughout the Pacific and included assignments to Southeast Asia. After completing his military service, Stanley achieved his MBA degree from Dartmouth University, specializing in operational logistics and process management.

Upon graduating Dartmouth University, Stanley was recruited by the venerable TBA Construction and Engineering Corporation, a 60-year-old international infrastructure and construction company. There Stanley began his tenure with the firm as Project Manager and was elevated to Executive Vice President of North American Operations within 3 years. He had overall responsibility for $170 million of projects at any given time. He directed more than 570 employees through 9 regional management executives that reported directly to him. He remained with TBA for 10 years and contributed to building the company into an international powerhouse with annual revenues exceeding $3.5 billion.

He then formed his own operations, logistics, and global expansion consulting firm for industry leaders and would-be industry leaders (Stanley & Associates International). He was immediately retained by TBA as a senior consultant, and his company began working with dozens of national and international companies in diverse industries including transportation, import-export, manufacturing, telecommunications, and health care. By the year 2000, SAI had 36 national and international clients, 96 employees (37 senior consultants), and annual revenues of $267 million.

Mr. Stanley has been an avid contributor to community projects and philanthropic activities with emphasis on youth advancement projects, the performing arts, and breast cancer research (finding "the cure"). He has personally, and through company involvement, contributed hundreds of thousands of dollars to help inner-city youth, expanded the performing arts in Michigan, and supported breast cancer research (his mother and sister passed away from breast cancer).

Fundamental to Lawrence Stanley's approach to business are his diverse life experiences, beginning with a multicultural and multilingual background, enhanced by six years of military training and experience. This is where he learned to fully appreciate the true values of discipline, focus, specialization, teamwork, and, above all else, leadership. His later experiences included complex logistics management and capitalizing multi-million-dollar projects. This demanded imagination, vision, and resourcefulness in his approach to high-profile, time-sensitive projects.

Stanley is a solution-driven professional. In an ever-changing global environment, Lawrence Stanley is best known for his leadership expertise in staying ahead of the curve and setting impressive benchmarks for others to follow. The ability to be fluidly flexible and responsive to changing markets and surround himself with world-class professionals have been hallmarks of Mr. Stanley's life as a businessman, husband, father, and proud citizen and servant of the United States Military.

CREATE A VIDEO RÉSUMÉ

Creating a video résumé is certainly a nontraditional strategy. A search for video résumés on *YouTube* will result in tens of thousands of candidates who have posted their video résumés for prospective employers to review. Many videos are well designed, while others are so poorly presented, they sabotage any chance of impressing a hiring professional. The advantage of a video résumé is that very few people have actually created one, so they serve as a differentiator in the recruiting process.

A good video résumé is short, describes the value you will bring to the job, and specifies how you will contribute to a company. An effective video résumé will quickly explain why you're the best person for the job and addresses your background in a story-like format. If you aren't a person with an outgoing and lively personality, don't come across well in a video, or cannot afford to produce a high-quality video, this may not be an appropriate tool for you. If you are going to consider this option, ensure that the content and presentation are professional and that the subject matter promotes you in an effective way.

CREATE AN EMPLOYMENT WEB SITE WITH YOUR OWN URL

Some job candidates opt to communicate more information than they can on their résumés, cover letters, and reference portfolios. An innovative solution is to create a job campaign Web site where you can include pictures and additional information, information that might not be appropriate on a résumé but that will help prospective employers get to know you better. The site might include more detailed references, project listings, accomplishments, and other *relevant information* that will provide added ammunition so you STAND OUT from competing job candidates. You can create a short Web site with your own URL that can be noted on your résumé so prospective employers can click through (obviously this is for e-mailed résumés) to your Web site to obtain this additional information.

Since you are working under the "no rules" philosophy, use common sense and include only information and material that is directly relevant to the hiring process, creating a Web site that will increase your job prospects. The Web site should be created the same way you created your résumé, so it serves as a means of communicating your value and ability to meet organizational goals and objectives. That being said, in the next chapter I will discuss the social networking site *LinkedIn*. Rather than going through the process of creating an individual Web site, you can set up a site on LinkedIn. The site will serve the same purpose, it is easy to create, and more and more hiring people are using LinkedIn to locate new hires. And there is no cost to you for establishing a presence on LinkedIn!

CASE STUDY PORTFOLIOS

The last communications tool is the case study portfolio. In the past, case study portfolios were developed primarily for senior-level management executives and professionals seeking positions at $150,000 and up. However, today, in troubled times and highly competitive job markets, case study portfolios are being used by anyone seeking a clear advantage in landing the best job opportunities. A case study portfolio is an employment tool that can best be described as a *mini interview*. Recall the *Law of Messaging* mentioned earlier in this chapter. You now know that about six to eight messages make 90 percent of the difference between getting an interview and not getting an interview, between getting a job offer and getting a rejection letter. When you identify those key six to eight performance messages, you will then come up with six to eight of the most impressive situations (case studies) that you encountered that would unquestionably demonstrate your professional competencies.

Challenge, Strategy, and Results

For each case study, you'll want to describe 1) the *challenge* you faced, 2) the specific *strategies* you used to successfully address the challenge, and 3) the *results* you achieved as a result of implementing the successful strategies.

A good length is a half page per case study, or two case studies per page. Developing a comprehensive, well-thought-out case study portfolio is important for a number of reasons: 1) It forces you to go back into your past work history and identify your greatest accomplishments, achievements, and contributions. Most people tend to take themselves and their victories in life and in their jobs for granted. 2) You will be a more powerful interviewee because you will have specific *cases* or situations you can talk about that will indicate to the interviewer that you can achieve significant results. 3) This is an innovative and notable tool to include with your résumé or as a leave-behind following an interview. Using a case study portfolio is yet another way to differentiate yourself from other qualified candidates seeking to win the job you want. For sure, 99.9 percent of your competition won't have one!

When to Use a Case Study Portfolio

If you are seeking a position at a yearly compensation level of $100,000 and above, you may want to consider including your cover letter, résumé, reference portfolio, and case study portfolio in one volume (hard copy or one electronic file). If you are pursuing a position that pays less than $100,000, you may want to consider including your cover letter, résumé, and reference portfolio but save your case study portfolio for the interview. It may be overkill to submit a case study portfolio for positions paying less than $100,000.

What follows are four sample case studies; each case study depicts a different profession or job. Study these samples, and then be creatively professional in developing your own portfolio.

Case Study for a Forklift Driver/Supervisor

THE CHALLENGE: DISORGANIZATION

I recognized that there were serious problems in the warehouse where restocking and order-picking activities interfered with each other. Neither activity was performed at optimal efficiency, not to mention the numerous forklift collisions, downtime and associated costs, and worker's compensation cases.

THE STRATEGY

I scheduled a meeting with the warehouse, shipping and receiving, and customer fulfillment managers. I described the chaotic, unproductive, and unsafe nature of operations. The warehouse looked like the Indianapolis Speedway—forklifts with incoming inventory racing to fill the bins competed for aisle space with forklifts racing to fill customer orders. I suggested a new logistical trafficking system that would result in an effective and safe environment. The warehouse floor was redesigned and color-coded to better control traffic flow and reduce accidents while improving efficiency and productivity.

THE RESULTS

Customer orders were filled 38 percent quicker, and the receiving and stocking of new merchandise improved 25 percent. Forklift accidents virtually ceased, saving the company over $600,000 a year (forklift repairs and worker's compensation claims).

Case Study for a Retail Manager

THE CHALLENGE: HIGH EMPLOYEE TURNOVER

I came to the realization that our high employee turnover was having a severe negative impact on sales and customer service at our prestigious fashion boutique on Worth Avenue in Palm Beach. Customers expected personalized attention from seasoned and established sales associates. Clients continually complained about the high turnover of employees and the inexperience and unprofessional nature of new associates.

THE STRATEGY

Corporate policy limited pay increases, so I developed a proposal for corporate to allow a 40 percent discount on all clothing purchased by our sales associates for themselves *and* for immediate members of their families (previously, employees were entitled to a 15 percent discount for themselves only). I also suggested that all sales associates receive a $250 bonus every six months they remained with the company—a loyalty gesture. I provided evidence that these changes would immediately pay for themselves as a result of increased sales and customer loyalty and retention.

THE RESULTS

A pilot program was implemented, and within six months, employee turnover was reduced from 87 percent to less than 11 percent, customer satisfaction skyrocketed, and sales increased 21 percent. The program was so successful, it was adopted nationally.

Case Study for a Secretary

THE CHALLENGE: OUTDATED PHONE SYSTEM AND POOR SERVICE

Customers were becoming irate. The phone system was so antiquated, customers were being left on hold too long, calls were being inadvertently disconnected, and tension throughout the office was reaching the boiling point. Management, however, was not overly enthusiastic about investing $60,000 in a new phone system.

THE STRATEGY

With the President's authorization, I went on *Craig's List* and eBay and began researching preowned phone systems, seeking out a viable system that would improve the company's efficiency while saving the company tens of thousands of dollars.

THE RESULTS

I located an Avaya Partner Telephone System set up for 15 lines and 40 phones or 12 lines and 32 phones—complete with all the state-of-the-art bells and whistles. The exact same system retailed new for $59,000 (including full installation). I negotiated a price of $9,800 and then located a local company that would install the entire system for $3,000. Along with a five-year warranty, this fully refurbished system saved the company $46,200 and played a significant role in improving efficiency and customer and employee satisfaction.

Case Study for a Chief Information Officer

THE CHALLENGE: NEED FOR NETWORK ADMINISTRATION

The company had no integrated IT network. Most of the information and data were kept on different programs or on employees' desktop computers. Information was not readily accessible. As a result, inefficiencies and under-productivity ran rampant. Timely delays were affecting everything including the bottom line.

THE STRATEGY

I coordinated a company server to be installed with Microsoft Office and 35 desktop computers with network capabilities. For the Accounting Department, QuickBooks Pro was installed. For the Sales Department a database in Access was designed and installed. The server also had remote access capability to provide senior management with up-to-date accounting information. Everyone was connected to everyone else.

THE RESULTS

Productivity was significantly improved, as key information was more readily available. Information that was partially inaccurate and took two days to access was now accurate and available in a matter of minutes. The Accounting Department estimated that these efforts in total saved the company over $800,000 a year.

CHAPTER 3 SUMMARY: BEST WAYS 46–70

46. Write a résumé that stands out from your competition. Your résumé must clearly communicate bottom-line results and organizational objectives you can produce that position you as a highly qualified and valuable candidate.

47. Write your résumé thinking about the interview. Think about the key messages you'll eventually want to communicate in an interview to win the job. When you take the time to properly prepare your résumé, thinking about the key messages that will win you job offers, you'll then showcase those messages on your résumé to win interviews!

48. There are no rules for writing résumés! The goal of your résumé is to STAND OUT. You cannot distinguish yourself from other job candidates if you blend in with them.

49. Keep your résumé as brief as possible. Given the scores of résumés crossing the desks of hiring authorities, shorter is better. A one- or two-page résumé is the norm, but *there are* exceptions.

50. Be careful not to conduct the interview in the résumé or ask the reader to labor through pages and pages of "stuff." Be precise, stay on message, and keep your résumé effectively succinct.

51. You must blow your own horn! Your résumé is not the place to be humble! It's the place to confidently show off past achievements and emphasize that you are the best candidate for the job!

52. Be sure your résumé is well organized and reader-friendly. The presentation should be crisp, exciting, and inviting.

53. When you have completed writing your résumé, test-market it! Identify five to seven people whose opinions you value and ask for their honest feedback. Also, when five to seven people read your résumé, this will assure you that there are no typographical or grammatical errors.

54. Don't lie. Be innovative and resourceful to get your foot in the door. But do so knowing you'd pass a lie detector test if you were asked about the truthfulness and accuracy of your résumé.

55. Your résumé must answer four critical questions. The first three must be answered in 15 to 20 seconds. The four questions are:

    a. What position(s) are you seeking or what are you qualified to do that would be of value to our company or organization?

    b. What results and contributions make you better than other qualified candidates?

    c. What skills, qualifications, and assets do you bring to the job that would lead us to believe you can produce the results you say you can produce?

    d. Can you provide specific results (achievements) that you produced in the past that would indicate that you can produce them in the future?

56. Know the Law of Messaging: *There are about six to eight messages that you have to communicate that make 90 percent of the difference between getting and not getting an interview.*

57. You will create a "showcase" atop your résumé. It is in the showcase where you will send your powerful 15-to–20-second message communicating that you are a highly qualified job candidate! In the showcase, include:

a. *The Ultimate Results messages.* The Ultimate Results messages communicate to prospective companies and hiring authorities your value, your worth to them. In other words, what you get paid to produce.

b. *The Core Strengths messages.* Determine and reveal your six to eight core strengths that would lead a prospective employer to believe you can produce the Ultimate Results.

c. *The Value-Added messages.* Value-Added messages communicate to prospective employers not only that you have the skills and qualifications to do the job better than other qualified candidates, but that you bring more to the job than what's required.

58. When you work on the employment section, you'll want to address two distinct components for each job or position that will appear on the résumé. 1) your detailed job responsibilities or job description and 2) your achievements and contributions—the results you produced.

59. Leave off personal information including age, place of birth, marital status, and other nonrelevant information on your résumé unless there is a strategic reason to include it.

60. Leave off all information relating to religious, political, and other possibly *controversial activities or subjects* on your résumé unless you have a valid reason to include such information.

61. As a rule, salary history is not included on résumés. If you are seeking a federal job or have other tactical reasons for including salary information, go ahead and include it.

62. You might want to consider including on your résumé the reasons for leaving places of employment. If you have had many jobs in a short period of time where you might be perceived

as an unreliable job candidate, you may want to provide short, effective, and nondefensive reasons for leaving prior positions.

63. Don't underestimate the intelligence of hiring and employment professionals. Do not come across as devious, deceptive, or desperate.

64. In addition to formal education, employers want to know what you do to continually expand your knowledge and improve your professional skills. What continuing education courses have you attended? How many personal development seminars have you completed? How many professional improvement workshops have you attended? What computer skills are you proficient in? Let employers know you are a lifelong student of your vocation.

65. If you have military experience, thank you for serving your country. I urge you to present your military experience on your résumé as proudly as you wore the uniform.

66. If you have space on your résumé and want to include relevant activities and professional affiliations, include them. If you are a member of professional associations, trade organizations, and business groups, include them.

67. Cover letters should be short, because most hiring authorities just don't have time to read lengthy cover letters. Cover letters should be personalized if possible.

68. The reference portfolio is the *secret weapon* of the job transition campaign. This tool is made up of professional references that will confirm and validate that the achievements and contributions you noted on your résumé are truthful and accurate.

69. Creating a video résumé is certainly a nontraditional strategy. If you choose to create one, be sure it is professional and well organized and will enhance your campaign.

70.   In tough economic times, consider using a case study portfolio. Case study portfolios give job candidates a clear advantage in landing the best jobs. A case study portfolio can best be described as a *mini interview*, and includes situations you faced in the past that demonstrate that you can meet challenges and solve problems expeditiously, professionally, and cost effectively. Each case study includes the *challenge*, the *strategy* used to confront the challenge, and the successful quantifiable *results* you attained based on your strategy.

CREATING A METICULOUS ACTION PLAN

DON'T LOOK EAST TO WATCH A SUNSET

At this juncture of the job transition process, I hope that you're excited about the prospects of landing a great job in any kind of economy or job market. By now, I am sure you have established and maintain a positive, energetic, and confident mindset, have identified a meaningful job or career objective, and have created and stockpiled a powerful arsenal of communications tools to outmaneuver and outcompete your competition. The next step of the job transition process is to take all this positive momentum and develop a Meticulous Action Plan (MAP) so you can pursue and land the job you want at the compensation you are worth.

TAKE OUT YOUR GPS DEVICE

Almost all of us seem to have a global positioning system (GPS) device these days in our cars, on our cell phones, or as a separate hand-held instrument. A GPS is a satellite-based navigation system that has many different applications. For instance, if you want to navigate your way around a golf course, GPS technology provides an accurate course map with "distances" to help you get from point A (the tee) to point B (the green). If you travel somewhere you've never been to, the GPS will provide a road map and precise directions for getting from your starting point to your ultimate destination. However, one of the limitations to GPS technology is that it does not have the capability of providing you with a road map that shows you how to go from unemployed to employed, or underemployed to gainfully employed. *This means you have to create your own MAP!*

PLANS

Successful endeavors are, in most cases, a result of following well-thought-out written action plans. A new business enterprise becomes a success because the owners had a well-conceived written business plan. The sports team wins because the coaches created a highly effective written game plan. Have you ever taken the time to think about all the written plans people write to achieve specific goals? There are retirement plans, vacation plans, financial plans, lesson plans, floor plans, weight loss plans, battle plans, wedding plans, recovery plans, flight plans, and emergency preparedness plans. *The truth of the matter is that when it comes to furthering your career, ensuring your family's financial well-being, and securing a meaningful and rewarding job, you need a MAP.* But if you're like 99.5 percent of all job seekers, you have no plan at all. And I remind you of the age-old cliché that *if you fail to have a written plan, you better plan to fail.*

The typical ineffective and painful job search is made up of two primary steps: 1) throw a résumé together, and 2) wing it! Winging it normally involves two approaches, *click and pray* and *lick and pray*. Click and pray is where you sit at your computer for hours on end and click your résumé out to hundreds, if not thousands, of employers and recruiters, praying that someone will read your résumé and offer you that perfect job. Lick and pray normally occurs on Sundays when you scour the classified advertisements. When you find jobs that interest you, you place your résumé in an envelope, lick it shut, deposit it in the mailbox, and pray someone will find your document in a stack full of competing résumés.

And then there is the matter of how much time the average out-of-work person invests in these two strategies during the week. The average unemployed job seeker spends less than 15 hours a week winging it! So let me pose a few questions to you. Do you know how many ways there are to land a job in troubled, uncertain job markets? Do you know which methods will work best for you? How many hours a week do you plan to invest in designing your future and landing your next job? What specific tasks will you work on each day? What are your goals for each week? Less than 1 percent of all job seekers ever ask these questions. So the good news is that if you're willing to roll up your sleeves and work hard to complete the assignments I will ask you to do throughout this chapter, you will find that securing the job you want in troubled, challenging times is not that difficult at all. *Once you have a well-designed written job transition strategy—a MAP—you'll have a clear advantage over 99.5 percent of your competition who are just winging it!*

THIS IS A WORKING CHAPTER

Simply reading this chapter won't help you much. The magic lies in completing the assignments I will ask you to complete. If you allow it to be, this can be an enjoyable and inspiring experience. *This is not homework; rather, it's designing your future work.* Once you have a plan of action that outlines daily tasks and weekly goals, you'll have created your own personal GPS that will direct you to your next job.

Without question, creating a sensible written strategy is more important than having a world-class résumé. As an example, let's take the case of Paul, who desperately needed a job. He had no résumé, but he did have a written strategy:

Paul's Written Strategy

Wake up every weekday at 7 a.m., get dressed, and eat a good breakfast.

At 9 a.m., head to Main Street, and call on businesses on Main Street and in office buildings all day, with the goal of calling on 60 to 80 businesses a day to land a job.

That was Paul's written MAP. His strategy was to wake up early every morning and spend the entire day walking down Main Street going into every store and office building, asking if anyone had any job openings. On his fourth day, with tired legs and having overcome one rejection after another, a company asked him to fill out an application, and Paul was hired two days later. Paul's strategy was the relentless pursuit of a job and a self-imposed demand that he call on 60 to 80 potential employers a day—or between 300 and 400 a week! How many people do you know who would do this? But Paul landed a job in a troubled and competitive job market in a matter of days, not weeks or months. Why? Because he had a highly effective written plan, as simple as it was, and he worked his plan highly effectively.

CREATING YOUR METICULOUS ACTION PLAN

Your MAP will be all encompassing and will address *your entire week's activities*. When you're done developing your action plan, you'll have a highly structured schedule of activities for each day of the week. This includes your job transition campaign as well as your personal, social, and fitness activities. MAPs are essential not only if you're out of work, but also if you have a job and are seeking a better one. If you are out of work, you can invest 50, 60, or 70 hours a week in your job transition campaign. If you have a full-time job, you may only have 5, 10, or 15 hours a week to invest in a job change campaign. Success is determined by 1) the number of hours you put into the job campaign and 2) the effort and activities you put into the hours. *Whether you are employed and looking for a better job or out of work seeking a new one, you must hold yourself fully accountable for putting in as many hours as possible and getting the most out of every hour you put in.*

How Many Hours a Week?

The first question you will need to address is, how many hours a week will you commit to your job transition campaign? If you are unemployed and must land a job quickly, 60 or more hours a week is *not* unreasonable. What else is more important if there's an urgency to get back to work? Personal responsibility and massive discipline are the two driving forces that will result in landing a job quickly when jobs are scarce. *Demand of yourself that you work hard, stay focused, and raise the bar so high, no other job candidate will match your level of intensity and activity.* When you work harder and smarter than your competition, you'll secure a new job with surprising ease in any kind of job market. If you currently have a job and are seeking a better opportunity, you must determine the number of hours you're able to invest each week. Ten hours is not unreasonable in most cases. Whether you are out of work or currently employed, at the end of each week, you must reflect upon the tasks you did and the goals you achieved. When you have a structured MAP, you'll have a powerful tool to motivate you and guide you each week, so you'll do all that you have to do to land a job in a troubled economy.

How Many Hours a Day?

Based on the number of *weekly* hours you'll invest in getting a new job, your next step is to break weekly hours down into *daily* hours. Below is a *conservative* strategy that I suggest to those job candidates who are out of work and have an urgency to gain new employment.

Number of Hours a Week: 50 Hours

Monday	9 hours
Tuesday	9.5 hours

Wednesday	9 hours
Thursday	9.5 hours
Friday	9 hours
Saturday	Off
Sunday	4 hours
Total:	50 hours

THE 13 WAYS TO GET A JOB

There are probably hundreds of ways to get hired. However, when broken down, there are 13 primary strategies for landing a job in troubled economic times with high unemployment.

1. *Networking and contact development*
   - The U.S. Department of Labor confirms that between 60 and 85 percent of all jobs are secured through networking, contacts you have developed or will develop who can refer you to people they know. *Networking, especially in troubled times, is, without question, the #1 way to get a new job.* Bob Burg, author of *Endless Referrals*, says, "Effective networking is a matter of utilizing your natural sphere of influence, together with the one you are creating through networking skills, so that you will be referred to those who can help you find the job you desire." You are not asking people in your network for jobs. You are asking people in your sphere of influence if they know of anyone in *their network* who can assist you to achieve your goal.
   - A relatively new, online networking technique is the use of social networks, particularly LinkedIn. *LinkedIn is an effective social networking site used almost exclusively for professional purposes including networking for new jobs and business opportunities.* Executive search firms use LinkedIn as a primary site for sourcing candidates. LinkedIn is an excellent networking strategy for online, non-face-to-face networking.

There are other social networking sites you can use such as Facebook, but use common sense when putting your sites together, and maintain a high degree of professionalism. Make sure your site is one that you'd be proud to show your mother!

2. *Target marketing (identifying companies you want to work for)*

   - Target marketing is a strategy for targeting specific companies or organizations you want to work for and proactively going after them! *Compile a list of 50 to a 100 companies you'd be interested in working for.* Then, research the name of the hiring manager for each company (sales director, accounting manager, customer service manager, warehouse manager, CEO, etc.). Once identified, send the person a *hard copy* of your cover letter, résumé, and reference portfolio by overnight or two-day delivery or by first-class mail. Be prepared to follow up by sending follow-up letters. Many unsolicited résumé files sent by e-mail won't make it through the firewalls or will be automatically deleted. However, most people eagerly open overnight delivery packages, and they'll eagerly open yours as well.

   - Susan J. Cook, executive vice president and chief human resources officer for Eaton Corporation, has some pointers from an HR perspective:

     > *Don't send résumés to multiple people in the same organization. Identify one person who would be the ideal person to read your résumé and send it to that person. Be professional and don't appear desperate. Respect the hiring manager's time. Also, don't send résumés to an executive and say you'll follow up in x number of days to schedule a meeting. They don't have time to take your call. Send a follow-up e-mail or letter if necessary. Research the company thoroughly and tell them how you can benefit them. If they have an open position and you communicate your value clearly, they will contact you.*

3. *Internet searches and postings*

   - You can use online job boards with access to millions of job openings posted by hiring companies and recruiters. Job candidates can enjoy many attractive benefits including online profiles, free résumé postings, and e-mail job alerts. In addition, most organizations now feature fully operational career sites that function much like online job boards. They also allow you to create profiles, subscribe to alerts, and respond to job openings. Hundreds and hundreds of job boards are available that serve a wide range of industries and professions.

   - Online communities, both large and small, are forums where like-minded individuals interact with each other. The large communities cater to millions of individuals with features such as news, job alerts, and company profiles. Smaller communities function as e-groups and e-lists, where members interact with each other on various issues. Executive recruiters and human resource professionals often target these groups to post openings and solicit résumés.

   - Online newspapers provide access to their employment classifieds and also to custom-designed job boards.

   - Web sites of industry associations function much like professional communities. In addition to links to members, they often offer forums, job boards, networking opportunities, and event announcements. If you are in a profession or vocation supported by strong industry associations, association Web sites will offer yet another vehicle to help you land your next job.

   - *Caution*: Conducting an online job transition campaign can be a highly effective strategy. *However, be aware that when you conduct an online campaign, you may be exposing yourself to potential privacy risks.* Your job campaign becomes transparent and is open to scrutiny by almost anyone. Always protect your personal information, and avoid disclosing your social security number and any confidential information. Know also that there are many employment scams and charlatans out there seeking to take advantage of job seekers' vulnerabilities during these troubled times, so be alert and use common sense and wise discretion. *And if you are employed, use extra caution if you don't want your current employer to find out that you're looking for a new job.* Extra care must always be taken if this is the case in *all* aspects of your campaign.

4. *Federal jobs*

   - Preparing a job campaign to land a federal job is different from preparing a job campaign in the private and nonprofit sectors. Kathryn Troutman, one of the nation's leading experts in federal job transitioning and author of *Ten Steps to a Federal Job*, says:

     > *Federal jobs are available across the U.S. and offer competitive salaries and benefits. No matter what your expertise or where you live, if you want a job where you can develop your professional skills and make a difference in the lives of others, check out federal employment. It's easy to find federal job announcements for any city in the United States and around the world at: www.usajobs.gov. You can search for jobs by geographic location, salary and job type.*

5. *Search firms and employment agencies*

   - Executive search firms and employment agencies get paid to place candidates in jobs. Normally, search firms place candidates in higher-level jobs, and employment agencies place candidates in low- to mid-range jobs, both permanent and temporary placements. The good news is that job candidates don't pay any fees. The not-so-good news is that *search and employment firms, as a rule, do not actively seek to place candidates; rather, they actively seek to fill client openings.* A common misconception is that recruiters and employment agencies are the personal placement agents for job candidates. They are not. They receive job vacancies from client companies and seek appropriate candidates to fill those slots—thus the term *headhunter*. Some agencies specialize in specific occupations, while others are more general. The best strategy regarding search firms and employment agencies is to use them for potential job openings and for information gathering, but don't count on them to be your savior!

6. *Blogs with job listings*

    • Today a good majority of people subscribe to blogs to receive information based on interests and relevant activities. Blogs help people obtain timely information to keep them updated on emerging or declining industry and market trends, as well as information that will help them make better decisions to achieve their goals. Recently, larger blogs are integrating job banks into their Web sites, and thus subscribing to blogs is becoming a new and emerging job transition strategy you may want to consider. Be careful of the time you spend blogging, and be sure that the time you spend is directly related to landing a job, not merely shootin' the breeze.

7. *Classified advertisements in newspapers and trade journals*

    • What used to be the primary method of securing employment is quickly going the way of the dinosaurs. During troubled economies and periods of high unemployment, job listings in the classified advertisement section are sparse at best. Yes, I suggest you get the Sunday newspaper and scan the classified section. But better yet, scan the entire newspaper and identify which companies are placing large ads. They may be good prospects to go after. Read the business section, and identify potential companies you may want to target-market (Strategy #2). Be proactive, perform in-depth research, and go after companies that seem to be doing well and that interest you.

8. *Job fairs*
    - Job fairs are a common method of entry-level recruiting and initial screening. They seldom provide a venue for significant mid-to upper-level jobs. For the corporate recruiter, they offer an opportunity to reach the most potential candidates in the shortest possible amount of time. For many students and entry-level candidates, job fairs provide an opportunity to meet with multiple employers in the same day. That being said, *one of the best strategies when attending job fairs is not to hand out résumés, but to collect as many business cards from the recruiters as possible.* Then, take them home, write a short, personal cover letter, and submit a hard copy of your résumé and reference portfolio by mail or overnight delivery. This way you STAND OUT from the rest of the crowd, and your résumé is not part of the job fair stockpile.

9. *College placement departments and alumni associations*
    - The primary goal of a college placement department is to provide students and alumni with the tools and skills they need to launch successful job campaigns to land fulfilling jobs. Though many institutions place more emphasis on inviting companies on campus to recruit students (give students a fish), more schools are beginning to teach the art of self-marketing and the job transition process (teach students how to fish). Many college and university alumni associations are seeing the value to helping former students find jobs and are offering services in that regard. This results in a win-win situation, where alumni associations help former students land jobs, which ensures that alumni contributions and donations keep rolling in from former students once they are successful.

10. *Workforce System and One-Stops*
    - The Workforce System is a network of federal, state, and local offices that support economic expansion, assist job seekers (mostly

unemployed) in securing employment opportunities, and train and develop talent to meet the skills, qualifications, and needs of the nation's employers. The Workforce System works in partnership with employers, educators, and community leaders to foster economic development and high-growth opportunities in regional economies. This system exists to help businesses find qualified workers and workers to find appropriate employers to meet their mutual needs.

- *The heart of the Workforce System is the One-Stop Career Center, the access point for qualified workers as well as federal, state, and local resources and assistance.* There are more than 3,000 One-Stop Career Centers located in all 50 states and Puerto Rico. One-Stop Career Centers place a multitude of resources for businesses and for job seekers under one roof. The typical One-Stop serves thousands of individuals who are seeking employment, changing jobs, reentering the workforce, or learning new skills. To start working with One-Stop Career Centers or to find out more about the services they offer, visit a One-Stop near you; go to www.servicelocator.org, or call 877-US2-JOBS.

11. *Volunteer work*

- When you volunteer, you feel better about yourself. You are doing something worthwhile when you help to improve the quality of life for others. And you have the opportunity to make new contacts that just might help you identify and land your next job. Volunteer to make a difference for others. Zig Ziglar said, "You can get anything you want out of life, if you help others to get what they want out of life."

12. *Job transition strategist*

- There is an emerging new occupation about to explode in the coming years. This new and emerging occupation is that of a job transition strategist. If employed workers want to secure new jobs but are working full weeks and have family obligations as well, they may want to hire a job transition strategist to send out résumés, make contacts, follow up on calls, and actually orchestrate and conduct the campaign for them. If out-of-work candidates require assistance in getting a new job, they may consider hiring a job transition strategist to work with them on their job transition campaign as well. This is a more expensive option, but I expect that this will soon become a significant new occupation. As is the case when hiring any professional, perform the due diligence, check references, and make sure you are working with a well-respected person or firm with a proven and reputable track record.

13. *Creative self-marketing*

- Creative self-marketing is just that—something that is unique, possibly outrageous, and different. Maybe you have the financial resources (and courage) to place your résumé in the newspaper as a full-page ad. Perhaps you have the financial resources (and courage) to purchase space on a billboard on a well-traveled road and advertise the position you are seeking. There is no limit to human creativity and resourcefulness. Creative self-marketing is "out-of-the-box" thinking about how best to land a job in challenging job markets.

SELECTING THE STRATEGIES THAT ARE BEST FOR YOU

Most likely, you won't use all 13 strategies. The strategies you decide to use will depend on the economy, your marketplace, the competition, your personality, finances, and other considerations. *Most effective action plans will incorporate 4 to 6 strategies. Your plan may include 3 strategies or 8. Ultimately, you must customize a MAP that will work best for you.* So review the 13 strategies, and determine which 4 to 6 strategies (or as many as you deem appropriate) will work most effectively for you. *Do not select strategies that are the easiest or most convenient.* Select those that, by working hard on them, will land the job you want no matter how tough the economy is or how competitive the job market may appear. Now, let's return to the weekly and daily hours discussed previously.

Number of Hours a Week: 50 Hours

Monday	9 hours
Tuesday	9.5 hours
Wednesday	9 hours
Thursday	9.5 hours
Friday	9 hours
Saturday	Off
Sunday	4 hours
Total:	50 hours

The next step is to determine what strategies you will undertake during the hours you allocate to your job transition campaign. Below is an example of how to do this.

Example

Rebecca is a real estate sales associate who lost her job. She decides to transfer her skills from real estate sales to health-care sales. Rebecca studied the 13 job transition strategies and determined she would use 6 of them. She committed to working 50 hours a week on her job transition campaign and decided to spend her time in the following way:

Networking	30%	15 hours a week
Target marketing	20%	10 hours a week
Internet activities	30%	15 hours a week
Employment agencies	5%	2 $1/2$ hours a week
Classified advertisements	5%	2 $1/2$ hours a week
Volunteer work	10%	5 hours a week
Total	100%	50 hours a week

Rebecca identified which strategies would produce the best results for her job campaign and determined how many hours to invest in each strategy. Now she needs to determine when, during the week, she will work her 15 hours of networking, 10 hours of target marketing, 15 hours of online work, 2 ½ hours with employment agencies and another 2 ½ on the classified ads, and 5 hours volunteering. Rebecca has come up with the following weekly action plan.

50 Hours per Week

	NETWORKING	TAR. MKT.	INTERNET	AGENCIES	CLASSIFIEDS	VOLUNTEER	TOTAL
Mon	3	4	2	0	0	0	9
Tue	4	0	4	1.5	0	0	9.5
Wed	4	4	1	0	0	0	9
Thu	4	2	2.5	1	0	0	9.5
Fri	0	0	4	0	0	5	9
Sat	Off	Off	Off	Off	Off	Off	Off
Sun	0	0	1.5	0	2.5	0	4
	15	10	15	2.5	2.5	5	50

Rebecca created a plan showing how she will spend her time and on what strategies for each day of the week. The plan can always be modified and tweaked. *But the objective is to produce a comprehensive MAP made up of specific activities that must be worked on every day to achieve the desired goal of landing a job quickly and methodically.*

TAKING CARE OF YOU IS JOB #1

While conducting your job transition campaign, *it is critically important that you take care of you first—physically and emotionally.* So the next step is to construct a highly *structured weekly schedule* that combines your job campaign efforts with activities not related to the job campaign, such as fitness, family time, and personal and social activities. Keep in mind that everything affects everything else. In the midst of a job transition campaign, you want to keep healthy and upbeat, to remain engaged with family members and friends, and to enjoy your hobbies and favorite activities to the extent that you can. If you enjoy golf but are on a tight budget, maybe you can play a round of golf once a month rather than every week, but practice once a week at the driving range to conserve your money. If you enjoy yoga but can't afford to go to class three times a week, maybe you can go once a week and purchase a video and practice at home the other two days until you land your next job and can return to the ideal regimen. You want to eat well, exercise every day (even if it's only a 30-minute walk), and stay happily engaged with family members and friends. Your *structured weekly schedule* will include both personal and job campaign activities. Look closely at Rebecca's *structured weekly schedule* below, and see how she successfully integrated personal and job campaign activities.

	MON	TUE	WED	THU	FRI	SAT	SUN
7:00	Exercise	Exercise	Exercise	Exercise	Exercise	Sleep late	Exercise
7:30	Exercise	Exercise	Exercise	Exercise	Exercise	Sleep late	Exercise
8:00	Breakfast	Breakfast	Breakfast	Breakfast	Breakfast	Sleep late	Breakfast
8:30	Shower/dress	Shower/dress	Shower/dress	Shower/dress	Shower/dress	Sleep late	Classifieds
9:00	Target mkting	Networking	Networking	Target mkting	Volunteer	Breakfast	Classifieds
9:30	Target mkting	Networking	Networking	Target mkting	Volunteer	Shower/dress	Classifieds
10:00	Target mkting	Networking	Networking	Target mkting	Volunteer	Yogaclass	Classifieds
10:30	Target mkting	Networking	Networking	Target mkting	Volunteer	Yoga class	Classifieds
11:00	Target mkting	Agencies	Networking	Agencies	Volunteer	Yoga class	Family time
11:30	Target mkting	Agencies	Networking	Agencies	Volunteer	Yoga class	Family time
Noon	Target mkting	Agencies	Networking	Internet	Volunteer	Family time	Family time
12:30	Target mkting	Internet	Networking	Internet	Volunteer	Family time	Family time
1:00	Lunch	Internet	Lunch	Lunch	Volunteer	Family time	Family time
1:30	Lunch	Lunch	Lunch	Lunch	Volunteer	Family time	Family time
2:00	Networking	Lunch	Target mkting	Networking	Lunch	Family time	Family time
2:30	Networking	Networking	Target mkting	Networking	Lunch	Family time	Family time
3:00	Networking	Networking	Target mkting	Networking	Internet	Family time	Family time

	Mon	**Tue**	**Wed**	**Thu**	**Fri**	**Sat**	**Sun**
3:30	Networking	Networking	Target mkting	Networking	Internet	Family time	Family time
4:00	Networking	Networking	Target mkting	Networking	Internet	Alone time	Family time
4:30	Networking	Family time	Target mkting	Networking	Internet	Alone time	Family time
5:00	Family time	Family time	Target mkting	Networking	Internet	Alone time	Family time
5:30	Family time	Family time	Target mkting	Networking	Internet	Alone time	Family time
6:00	Family time	Family time	Family time	Family time	Internet	Alone time	Family time
6:30	Family time	Internet	Family time	Family time	Internet	Alone time	Family time
7:00	Family time	Internet	Family time	Family time	Family time	Alone time	Family time
7:30	Internet	Internet	Family time	Family time	Family time	Time w/ friends	Family time
8:00	Internet	Internet	Family time	Internet	Family time	Time w/ friends	Internet
8:30	Internet	Internet	Internet	Internet	Family time	Time w/ friends	Internet
9:00	Internet	Internet	Internet	Internet	Family time	Time w/ friends	Internet

YOUR ACTION PLAN IS YOUR BOSS

If you are out of work, your job transition campaign must be a full-time activity. If you are currently employed seeking a new job, your job campaign must be treated like a part-time job. In both scenarios, you are the transition technician, and your MAP is the boss! When you look at Rebecca's weekly plan, almost every minute of the week is accounted for. Does this seem overly structured to you? *This is what it takes to land a job quickly in a troubled and high unemployment market.* Indeed, there is room for flexibility. You may need to rearrange your schedule as a result of "stuff" that will come up in the course of a week. But at the end of the week, your boss (your action plan) requires that you work so many hours on specific strategies. Do not let yourself off the hook. If anything, do more than the boss requires!

GOAL SETTING

All the planning in the world will lead you nowhere if you don't have clearly defined goals. Jim Cathcart, award-winning motivational speaker, said, "Most people aim at nothing in life and hit it with amazing accuracy."

However, when you create your action plan, you create a big target you can aim at and hit with amazing accuracy!

Once you have a *structured weekly schedule*, you must set goals that you want to achieve from your weekly activities. I have five principles for goal setting, and all five principles must be followed so that your future efforts lead to a well-paying job in the shortest amount of time possible.

1. *Set the bar high.* Resist the easy button. *Choose "mastery" over "easy"* and know that great accomplishments don't come from low expectations.

2. *Be realistic.* You want to set the bar high but not so high that your goals are merely impossible dreams. Don't ever settle for less, but be realistic when setting the bar high, especially when it comes to timelines and deadlines. In most cases, there are no such things as unrealistic goals, just unrealistic timetables for their achievement.

3. *Don't cave in.* It's easy to get distracted. It's easy to let influences pull you away from your *structured weekly schedule* in pursuit of your goals. Discipline and resolve will lead to your next job. Don't cave in on the high expectations you establish for yourself when you set the bar high (above in Principle #1).

4. *Don't substitute.* Carroll O'Connor, the late actor who played the role of Archie Bunker in the sitcom *All in the Family*, said that *the problem for most people is that when they meet resistance in pursuit of their goals, they substitute easier goals rather than create better plans.* When you meet resistance in pursuit of your goals (and you will), do not substitute easier goals; rather, create a more refined plan or work harder at the one you have.

5. *Celebrate.* When you achieve goals, celebrate! You work hard to achieve your goals, so when you achieve your weekly objectives, celebrate. If your goal is to send out 50 résumés a week and you meet that goal, celebrate even though you haven't landed a job yet. You are celebrating the achievement of sending out 50 résumés. When you celebrate, you appreciate and honor your own efforts. And when you begin to

fully appreciate your own efforts, you will begin to achieve the goals to which you aspire.

Rebecca's Goals

Rebecca's goals are outlined in detail below. These goals are based on the *structured weekly schedule* she created earlier.

Weekly Goals

Networking

- 5 new contacts referred by people in my network
- 2 new contacts made on my own
- 3 to 5 follow-up communications from contacts made the previous week
- 3 to 5 follow-up communications from contacts made in the last month
- 1 weekly e-mail message sent to all contacts via my LinkedIn site

Target marketing

- 15 unsolicited résumés to be sent out
- 10 to 15 follow-up letters and e-mails for résumés sent out last week
- 15 to 20 follow-up letters and e-mails for résumés sent out in the past month
- 5 phone calls to companies I'd really like to work for

Internet

- Review positions posted on Craigslist, Monster.com, hotjobs.yahoo.com, and Careerbuilder.com
- 25 résumés submitted online
- 10 or more postings on job boards; update existing postings
- Update my own LinkedIn site weekly

Employment agencies

- 3 to 5 contacts
- 3 to 5 follow-up communications (letters, e-mails, or faxes).

Classified advertisements

- 1 to 3 résumés to be sent responding to ads seen in the classified section
- 3 to 5 résumés to be sent out unsolicited based on scanning the entire Sunday newspaper(s)

Volunteer

- Have fun and contribute in a meaningful way to a cause I believe in
- Meet as many new people as I can, and *authentically* establish new relationships

Personal

- Enjoy every day, and smile throughout the day no matter what
- Reward myself with a martini only after I achieve my daily goals
- Walk 45 minutes every morning, 6 days a week
- Read a spiritual book 30 minutes every night before I turn on the television
- Call a friend at the end of every day to stay "connected"
- Have a "fun night out" every Saturday night with my spouse and friends
- Limit television (or eliminate it completely); watch only uplifting shows
- Eat well, take vitamins, and stay energetic and fit

Suppose I asked you to play a sport you never heard of. You arrive on the field, and I give you dozens and dozens of activities you have to do, but I don't tell you the goal of the game. If you don't know the goal of the game, how can you possibly win? If you have a *structured weekly schedule* but no goals, how can you win the job you want, especially during troubled economic times? So the final and most important part of designing an inspiring, high-powered MAP is setting specific goals.

Again, as Carroll O'Connor suggested, if your goals are not being attained, you don't compromise or give up on your objective of landing a job; you modify your plan. *The action plan is your road map or "ticket" to your next job.* The great Italian painter and sculptor, Michelangelo, said, "I hope that I always desire more than I can accomplish." Put your desires in writing, set the bar high, and follow the five principles of goal setting. When you do, you'll be employed before you know it!

Assignment: It is now time for you to put quality time into creating your own customized MAP. Please go back and review the 13 strategies, and then prepare a plan that you will commit to and enjoy executing!

My Meticulous Action Plan (MAP)

Number of weekly hours:

_____

Number of hours per day:

_____

- Monday

_____

- Tuesday

_____

- Wednesday

_____

- Thursday

_____

- Friday

_____

- Saturday

_____

- Sunday

_____

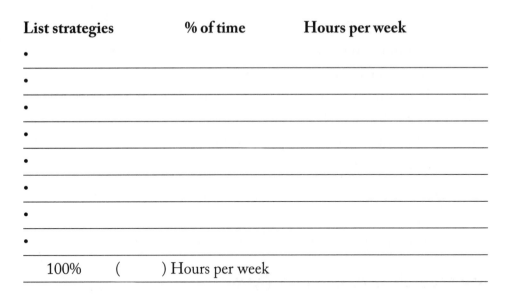

List strategies	% of time	Hours per week
•		
•		
•		
•		
•		
•		
•		
•		

100%   (   ) Hours per week

Once you have identified the specific strategies you will use to conduct your job transition campaign, determine the percentage of time you want to devote to each strategy. Then you can determine the number of hours a week you will work at each. For instance, suppose you plan to invest 60 hours a week on your campaign, and 25 percent of that time will be spent on networking; 25 percent of 60 hours is 15 hours. If you are employed and can only invest 9 hours a week on your campaign where 60 percent will be spent contacting search firms and 40 percent networking, you'd spend 5 $\frac{1}{2}$ hours on the former and 3 $\frac{1}{2}$ hours on the latter.

STRUCTURED WEEKLY SCHEDULE

Create you own personalized *structured weekly schedule* so you have a well-thought-out plan of action, knowing exactly what tasks you will perform each day. Include job campaign, personal, fitness, social, and all weekly activities.

	Mon	Tue	Wed	Thu	Fri	Sat	Sun
7:00							
7:30							
8:00							
8:30							

	MON	TUE	WED	THU	FRI	SAT	SUN
9:00							
9:30							
10:00							
10:30							
11:00							
11:30							
Noon							
12:30							
1:00							
1:30							
2:00							
2:30							
3:00							
3:30							
4:00							
4:30							
5:00							
5:30							
6:00							
6:30							
7:00							
7:30							
8:00							
8:30							
9:00							
9:30							
10:00							

Notes:

Weekly Goals

Strategy #1

-
-
-

-
-

Strategy #2

-
-
-
-
-

Strategy #3

-
-
-
-
-

Strategy #4

-
-
-
-
-

Strategy #5

-
-
-
-

Strategy #6

-
-

- _____
- _____
- _____

Strategy #7 _____

- _____
- _____
- _____
- _____

Strategy #8 _____

- _____
- _____
- _____
- _____
- _____

DON'T IGNORE THE TOUGH STUFF

It stands to reason that you will create and modify your action plan based on many different variables, such as your finances, health issues, geography, market economics, and personality. But in the event your plan doesn't produce the results you want as quickly as you anticipate, you need to be proactive by planning a strategy that addresses the _worst-case scenario._

Yes, it is vitally important to remain in a positive, optimistic, and enthusiastic state of mind. This was thoroughly discussed in Chapter 1. But we all know that bad things can happen to good people and that Murphy's law is real! So here's a good philosophy you might want to adopt: _expect the best, but plan for the worst._

Create the most powerful, aggressive, and results-driven MAP you can to land the job you want and deserve. But also spend just a little time thinking about the worst-case scenario. This would include taking an honest look at your finances and planning how best to navigate through a longer-than-expected campaign. Be open with family members and friends, and muster the courage and resilience to face what must be faced to best serve and protect you and your family.

To effectively address the worst-case scenario, you might include seeking out employment professionals and professional help in any area that might affect your ability to launch a hard-hitting and effective job transition campaign. You might need to consider moving in with relatives for a short period of time to save money. Not ideal, *but a bridge to your next opportunity*. You might have to find a part-time job even though this is not high on your "this-is-what-I-want-to-do" list.

Perhaps you need to develop a life downsizing plan. Just as many businesses are downsizing, so must many individuals and families. This doesn't have to be painful. Can't you have fun figuring out how to cut back on things you really don't need or use so you can put more money in your pocket instead of lining the pockets of others? Ask yourself, "How can I downsize my life, enjoy the process, and still live a good quality life?" If you ask that question with the sincere desire to answer it, with enthusiasm and passion, you'll come up with the answer. As the Good Book says, "Ask and you shall receive."

An effective action plan does not ignore potential obstacles. You can't take the chance that potential obstacles won't become very real barriers to achieving your goal. They will. I previously shared with you the Law of Ignoring, which says that whatever you ignore will, in most cases, get worse in time or will come back to bite you in the you-know-where. Any number of obstacles might exist, including insufficient experience, educational and academic deficiencies, a lack of cutting-edge skills, the real but never admitted discriminations (age, disability, gender, race, etc.), an extended absence from the workplace, and an erratic work history. You must address and neutralize these obstacles. If you are not sure how to accomplish this, seek out counsel from job coaches, employment professionals, the dedicated people at the Workforce One-Stops, books, and "timely and relevant" information found online (keeping in mind that there is a lot of misinformation online).

SUMMARY

Anything is possible if you are committed to it! An action plan that is well developed and well thought out will become your GPS to your next job in a troubled economy and highly competitive job market. When you know what you're going to do and accomplish every day of every week, your job campaign won't last very long. Yes, "winging it" is a strategy. It's just not a good one; in fact, it is usually a long and painful one. You should be thrilled knowing that if you put the time and energy, the thought and enthusiasm, into designing a customized MAP, you will be light-years ahead of your competition. You'll be enjoying your first annual performance review while your competition is still clicking, licking, and praying!

CHAPTER 4 SUMMARY: BEST WAYS 71–80

71. When it comes to ensuring your family's financial well-being, and securing a meaningful and rewarding job, you need to create a written action plan or a MAP (Meticulous Action Plan).

72. When you create a MAP, you are actually programming your own "employment GPS" so you can go from where you are to where you want to be.

73. When you're done developing your action plan, you'll have a highly structured schedule of activities for each day of the week. This includes your job transition campaign as well as your personal, social, and fitness activities.

74. If you are unemployed, you should invest 50, 60, or 70 hours a week on your job campaign. If you have a full-time job, you need to set aside a defined number of hours every week as your investment in your future.

75. Whether you are employed and looking for a better job or out of work seeking a new one, you must hold yourself fully

accountable for putting in as many hours as possible and getting the most out of every hour you put in.

76. The first question you will need to address is, how many hours a week will you commit to your job transition campaign? Then, based on the number of *weekly* hours you'll invest in getting a new job, your next step is to break weekly hours down into *daily* hours.

77. There are 13 primary job transition strategies for landing a job in troubled economic times. Your job is to determine which 4 to 6 strategies will be most effective for you.

   a. Networking and contact development
   b. Target marketing (identifying companies you want to work for)
   c. Internet searches and postings
   d. Federal jobs
   e. Search firms and employment agencies
   f. Blogs with job listings
   g. Classified advertisements in newspapers and trade journals
   h. Job fairs
   i. College placement departments and alumni associations
   j. Workforce System and One-Stops
   k. Volunteer work
   l. Job transition strategists
   m. Creative self-marketing

78. Once you have identified which job transition strategies will work best for your campaign, determine when, during the week, you will work on each. You want to create a *structured weekly schedule*. When you create a *structured weekly schedule*, you will have a detailed plan with specific

daily tasks both for your job campaign and for personal and social activities.

79. Once you have a *structured weekly schedule*, you must set goals that you want to achieve from your weekly activities.

   A MAP without specific goals is not an effective plan. You will want to set specific goals for each strategy so you can track your success or modify the MAP if you are not achieving your weekly goals.

80. Prepare for the *worst-case scenario*. It is vitally important to remain in a positive, optimistic, and enthusiastic state of mind. But sometimes your plan won't come to fruition as quickly as you'd like. So *expect the best, but plan for the worst*. This would include looking at your long- and short-term finances and health and other issues that need to be addressed to free you up to concentrate on getting your next job.

CHAPTER

5

TAKING ACTION

"AS YE SOW, SO SHALL YE REAP"

"**P**ut your money where your mouth is." "Actions speak louder than words." This chapter is the miracle piece of the job transition process. If you have a positive attitude, a well-defined goal, a strong résumé and other communication tools, and a well-thought-out action plan, but you take no action, you get no results—no new job. Contrary to popular belief, knowledge is *not* power. *Knowledge is potential power.* Power and success come from taking action on what you know.

TAKE ACTION AND ESTABLISH YOUR CAMPAIGN HEADQUARTERS

Do not minimize the importance of having an inspiring place from which to conduct your job transition campaign. You want to be working in an organized and efficient environment that feels good and motivates you. *You will be more productive if you headquarter your campaign from a home office or some location other than your kitchen table.* You'll want to direct your campaign and take action from a place that empowers you to work hard and intelligently, one that provides access to a computer, printer, the Internet, a fax machine, and a filing system. You'll need privacy to think and to focus on your daily tasks and objectives. Perhaps you can create a home office. Or possibly you'll use the public library as your campaign headquarters. The point is that your job transition campaign office must be similar to a political campaign headquarters—functional, motivating, and highly productive. If you enjoy going to a productive and comfortable campaign headquarters every day, your campaign will be a successful one, and you'll land the job you want sooner than you think.

TAKE ACTION AND DRESS TO WIN!

In the same way an inspiring headquarters enhances your job campaign, the way you dress also determines the way you feel, your productivity, and your outcome. Waking up in the morning and working on getting a job while you are wearing your pajamas isn't the action you want to take that will put you in a peak-performing state of mind. You wouldn't show up to work for an employer in your underwear, and you shouldn't show up working on your next job dressed like that either. During the day, you want to dress as if you will meet your next employer at any time. Look and feel professional. Of course, if you're going to spend time at night on the Internet working from home, you can dress down. Keep in mind *that what you wear determines how you feel and that how you feel determines the level of success you will achieve.* When you work on your job transition campaign, dress to win!

TAKE ACTION AND IMPLEMENT YOUR METICULOUS ACTION PLAN

It's been said that most people know what to do but their lack of success is a result of not doing what they know. I hope by now you have a detailed action plan with your *structured weekly schedule* of tasks and goals. Now, you simply need to hold yourself accountable to meet the demands of each day. Don't neglect to work your plan. In fact, every day, go the extra mile on behalf of your better future. *At a time where most of your competition will do the bare minimum, make sure you always demand more of yourself.* Take action to implement your MAP. Massive action leads to massive results!

TAKE ACTION TO ELIMINATE OBSTACLES TO SUCCESS

It is important that you remain laser-focused on your campaign; you want no distractions. If you are experiencing financial challenges, take action and seek out a financial adviser, your accountant, family members, or friends who can help you address and overcome this obstacle. If you have health issues, take action and get medical advice from appropriate sources to best resolve or work through your issues. If you've lost your health insurance, seek advice from a trusted insurance professional, visit one of the many free health clinics located throughout the country, or visit a medical center or your doctor and ask for suggestions. *Every problem has a solution if you are committed to finding one.* If you have personal problems that are consuming your thoughts and time, take action and go for counseling, vent to a friend, or find the proper resources to assist you with your concerns. *The take-home message here is that you need to invest 100 percent of your resources and energy in implementing your action plan to land the job you want in tough job markets and troubled economies.* So take the necessary action to avoid any distractions that will impair your campaign.

TAKE ACTION TO ACCESS TECHNOLOGY

The Internet provides critical information in a timely manner that is necessary to land a job in any job market, especially a troubled economy with high unemployment. *It is required that you have access to a computer and the Internet.* Many companies and organizations won't accept résumés unless submitted electronically. It's also important to be skilled in the use of the latest technologies and software. Cover letters need to be personalized, résumés must be tweaked for differing job requirements, and short but personalized thank-you e-mails or letters must be sent out after each interview and network meeting. Most libraries provide computer services and Internet access if you don't have your own. Perhaps you can make arrangements to use the computer of a family member or friend, so long as you have privacy and the ability to focus on the tasks at hand. Take action to gain access to the technology you'll need to land a job in today's technology-driven society and job market. Take action and learn a few simple applications, such as Internet research, MS Word, and e-mail capabilities so you can optimize your efforts and get the most out of today's technology to get a new job sooner rather than later.

TAKE ACTION TO DEVELOP YOUR PERSONAL SALES FORCE

Let's use common sense and look at the realities of how most jobs are filled in a troubled economy. In a competitive market with high unemployment and discontent among many employed workers, a good majority of job openings are filled with people who know the hiring managers or who are in the hiring manager's sphere of influence. In other words, a good percentage of jobs are never advertised or are filled before they're advertised. This way of acquiring jobs is often referred to as the *hidden job market,* even though it is not hidden at all. The term simply means that job openings are filled through the networking process. No doubt, many people cringe at the idea of having to network, but like it or not, in highly competitive job markets it's still who you know more than what you know. I discussed networking briefly in the last chapter but feel compelled to spend a bit more time on this subject because, in troubled economies, networking is more important than ever.

Networking can be enjoyable because you're actually developing your own personal sales force! Remember, you are not asking people you know for a job. Rather, you are asking them to tap into their network of people to access someone they know who can assist you in landing a job. Max

Messmer, CEO of Robert Half International, Inc., one of the world's largest specialized staffing firms, says that "the biggest mistake most job seekers make when it comes to networking is not doing enough of it. The vast majority of jobs—as many as 80 percent by most estimates—are filled today by people who first heard about a job opportunity informally, through another person. So no matter how many people you have in your network, it's never enough."

Just about everybody knows at least 200 people: family, friends, the dry cleaner, the dentist, neighbors, and so on. If 200 people know 200 people, you have a potential network, or sales force, of 40,000 people! And even if everybody you know just knows 100 people, this represents a network, or sales force, of 10,000 people. Messmer also suggests that "you must add new contacts to your network every week; 10 new contacts a week is not an unreasonable goal." If 10 new people know 200 people, that's an additional 2,000 potential contacts added to your network every week!

Tim Best, principal and senior vice president of client services for Bradley-Morris, Inc., one of the nation's largest military job placement recruiters, says:

> *Get LinkedIn! Build a professional and complete profile with the same care and concern you would build your résumé. Then utilize this wonderful networking tool to introduce yourself to actual decision-makers. You don't have the ability to just randomly contact anyone in LinkedIn, but you can request introductions through people you know and this is an excellent way to get "referred" to someone in a hiring mode. Also, network with association leaders. Almost every industry has an association, or multiple associations, that assists in matching qualified association members seeking work with industry employers. This is becoming a primary member benefit especially in tight job markets. You'll be pleasantly surprised how cooperative most association leaders are in providing information to help you secure a new job!*

When you speak with a networking contact by phone or in person, you want to be sure you leave the conversation achieving one or more of the following objectives:

1. Advice and information that will help you conduct a more efficient, effective, and focused campaign

2. An introduction to someone who knows of an existing job opening

3. The name of a recruiter, a company, or an organization that might be seeking a person with your skills and qualifications

4. Referrals to people who may know other people who can help you identify and secure employment opportunities

5. A follow-up meeting or phone conversation with your contact, providing additional leads or information after your contact has had time to go through his or her list of contacts

When you speak with people from your network, be specific about what you want from them. Don't waste their time or put them in an uncomfortable position. "Help, I'm looking for any kind of job" won't work in most cases. "I am seeking your advice and information on how best to secure an entry-level accounting position in telecommunications or any high-tech environment. Any help you might be able to provide would be greatly appreciated" is a much more effective approach. Be respectful of their time. Be precise in communicating what kind of help you are seeking.

Caution: Do not back your contacts into a corner by asking for a job. By doing so, you place them in an uncomfortable and awkward position, and they'll avoid you from that point on. *The networking process is one where you are seeking advice and information.* Offer to provide a résumé, and following your discussions with your contacts, always send or e-mail a thank-you note.

You can't avoid networking in troubled times. Actually, you can't avoid networking in favorable economies and job markets either. Keep in mind that networking is synonymous, not with begging for a job, but rather with creating your own sales force to assist you in connecting with your next employer.

TAKE ACTION TO ACE THE INTERVIEW

You can't afford to blow the sale; you've come too far. You worked hard to stay positive throughout the job campaign. You defined your goal, created your résumé, and produced powerful communication tools. You developed a well-designed MAP and implemented your action plan with meticulous precision. Now comes the moment of truth. After all the positive and enthusiastic energy invested in your job transition campaign, it all comes down to the interview. And you must be as well prepared for the interview as presidential candidates are for their televised debates!

The interview is an equal encounter between two parties—one who has a position to fill and one who wishes to fill that position. Unquestionably, one of the greatest human fears is that of public speaking. This would help explain why so many people have a fear of interviews. An interview is nothing more than a public speaking engagement in a private setting. In fact, it's more challenging because interviewees (job seekers) have not been given their scripts for the interview. They don't always know what will be asked or what to expect. And in addition to the fear of public speaking, another significant reason most people are uncomfortable in an interview is that they feel they are being judged. They don't view an interview as a two-way, equal conversation. They feel totally vulnerable.

Then, there are those job candidates who believe they interview well. The truth of the matter is that these people do feel comfortable interviewing and are able to build good rapport and communicate well. But the fact is, in most cases, they do not differentiate themselves from other qualified candidates. They do not communicate what value-added benefits they bring to the job that makes them highly qualified. They do not blow their own horn loud and clear. The general consensus among the majority of hiring professionals is that most job seekers are not prepared enough for interviews, undersell themselves, and fail to make a clear case for why they are the best candidates for the job.

The Interview Is a Meeting

The employment interview is just a meeting. Although you shouldn't, by any means, treat this meeting lightly, you must keep in mind that there is a mutual need. You need a job, and the company or organization needs an employee. In fact, it's possible the organization interviewing you may need you more than you need a job! So the key to acing the interview is to be well prepared. There are two important aspects to being well prepared: 1) you need to be prepared to convince the interviewer that you can do the job as well as or better than other candidates, and 2) you need to be prepared to convince the interviewer that you're a good fit for his organization.

You Can Do the Job as Well as or Better Than Other Candidates

One of the habits that Dr. Stephen Covey discusses in his book *7 Habits of Highly Effective People* is, "Seek first to understand, then to be understood." I'm not sure preparing for an interview can be summed up any better. You must know what the company's needs are. You need to know what the organization's problems are. You must know what the company's goals and objectives are. And then you need to blow your own horn confidently, not arrogantly, and convince interviewers that you understand the company's needs. You must persuade them that your presence at the interview is primarily to demonstrate, beyond any doubt, that you can meet their needs, solve their problems, and help them achieve their goals.

Hiring professionals want to know if you've done your homework and are knowledgeable about their company's products, services, history, reputation, leadership, and so on. Yes, it's a one-way courtship at first. But once a company or an organization sees how much you know about it, it will want to know all about you. So, know the company, know the job you are interviewing for, know the industry the company is in, and know your most valuable skills qualifications and abilities that will convince a prospective employer that you are the best candidate for the job.

You're a Good Fit

Once you have proved that you are qualified and capable of doing the job, the final piece to the interviewing puzzle is indicating to the interviewer that you are a good fit for the company or organization. People hire people they feel comfortable with and those who share common values. Said differently, *people hire people they like.* You must arrive at the interview knowing the company's values and culture. In most cases, this information is easily accessible on the company's Web site. If, for instance, you know that a company's values include honesty and integrity and going the extra mile to provide groundbreaking levels of customer service, you must communicate that you share these traits during the interview. If a friend works for the company you are interviewing with and informs you that the company expects its employees to work late hours and occasional weekends, if you want a job offer, you must let the interviewer know, during the interview, that you are willing to work long hours, including weekends. Other characteristics that might make up a company's culture include dress code, personality, pace, social interaction, and industry commitment. A good fit means you've matched your personal characteristics to those of the company you are interviewing with.

Behavioral-Based Questions

More and more interviewers are conducting behavioral-based interviews. Actually, "case study" interviews would better describe this type of interview. A behavioral-based interview is made up of open-ended questions that ask you to illustrate and explain actual circumstances that you have previously faced. The interviewers want you to detail specific events, projects, or situations you've encountered in the past and the skills and intellect you used to address them. And, of course, they want to know the results you produced and contributions you made. Behavioral-based interviews predict future performance based on past performance. For candidates new to the job market, such as college graduates or first-time workers, behavioral-based questions may be hypothetical and "what-if" inquiries such as, "If this were to occur while on the job, how would you react?" or "If you experienced a problem working with a peer, what steps would you take to resolve the problem?"

In truth, behavioral-based interviews are more enjoyable and provide you with more control of the interview than you might realize. You have greater control because you can both answer the behavioral-based question and provide additional information that you feel is valuable to differentiate you from your competition. Haven't you watched presidential debates where a candidate is asked a question where he answers it quickly and then moves on to a completely different and unrelated subject? He does this intentionally because he wants to take control of the debate (interview) by addressing what he feels the audience wants to hear. This is how he gets elected (hired). And this is how you get hired in troubled times beset with high unemployment. You must address the subjects and issues that you know interviewers need to hear to tip the scale in your favor.

Behavioral-based interviews are the forum to *seal the deal!* Be fully prepared. Come into the interview knowing your value and how you can benefit the company. And come prepared with stories, examples, and case studies to offer evidence that you are qualified for the job. Be honest, confident (again, not arrogant), and authentic. Go into the interview expecting to enjoy an informative two-way discussion. Let me share with you five important tips so you can enjoy the process and interview effectively:

1. *Be prepared for tough questions.* Anticipate, in advance, those questions that are uncomfortable for you. Then, script out answers so you become totally comfortable with them. Don't be caught off guard!

2. *Don't let unlawful questions rattle you.* Ellen Block, my wife and an employment law attorney, says:

> *Unlawful interview questions are questions that are not directly job-related which attempt to elicit information about race, color,*

ancestry, age, gender, religion, and/or disability, unless based upon bona fide occupational qualifications. If you are asked such a question, you should professionally and tactfully ask the interviewer about the business-basis for the question before you answer. For example, if asked your age, you could respond by saying, "I'm happy to answer your question, but can you clarify for me the business reason for your question?" or if you are asked "What church do you attend?" you may reply by saying, "In preparation for my interview today, I thoroughly reviewed the qualifications and I admit I was not prepared to answer that question as church attendance was not listed as a qualification. But if this position requires it, I will be happy to answer." Understandably, this is not easy or comfortable to say for many people, but your honesty and respectful straightforwardness may just gain you points in the interview. However, if an unlawful question is asked for a seemingly well-intentioned reason and it does not offend you or cause a hiring concern, stay cool and just answer it in an effective and confident way. The goal is to win the job offer. Then, based on how you feel after you've been offered the job, you determine if you'll accept it or not.

3. *Be prepared to ask good questions.* Hiring professionals are placing more and more weight on the quality of the questions you ask them in interviews. Prepare four or five intelligent, provocative, and sensible questions that will indicate you take the interview as seriously as they do.

4. *Be ready to handle the subject of salary.* If the subject of salary comes up during the interview, the general rule is to try and avoid it until an offer has been made. This is because the greatest leverage you have is after the job offer but before acceptance. However, you may have no choice but to discuss salary when asked about your salary requirements or salary history. You must know, in advance, the salary range for the job you are seeking and then provide a realistic range; "I would expect the job to pay between $30,000 and $40,000, and I believe, based on my value

to your company, we can agree to an amicable number." Or "Over the past five years, my salary has been between $80,000 and $93,000. I plan to make a significant contribution to your sales efforts, so my starting salary is less important than the ability to demonstrate to you that I can produce results. And I am sure when you see the results I can produce, my salary will reflect those contributions." Once again, I emphasize that if you know your value and how you can contribute in a notable way, you'll feel in control when negotiating a win-win compensation arrangement.

5. *Follow up.* First and without exception, always mail or e-mail a thank-you note within hours following an interview. Unless you have a reason to do otherwise, keep the message short and subtly show your interest to move forward in the hiring process. "Thank you for taking the time to meet with me this afternoon. I am confident that I am highly qualified for this job and look forward to the next step in the hiring process." After the interview, maintain professional contact with the interviewer. If the interviewer tells you that you'll be contacted in a week, wait the full week. If you don't hear back in a week, a phone call or e-mail is appropriate. Stay in touch with the interviewer, but also be keenly aware of that fine line between staying in touch and being a nuisance—and don't cross it.

BACKGROUND CHECKS

Andrew J. Tabone, manager of IT, Recruitment & Career Development for Carnival Cruise Lines, says:

> *Preemployment criminal background, credit, and drug tests are requisite conditions for most full-time positions as well as for temporary contract engagement work, especially in times of high unemployment. This is no longer reserved for larger employers these days. In addition to impeccable employment references, situations occur where candidates may success-fully make it through the rigors of applying for, interviewing for, and*

CRESTWOOD PUBLIC LIBRARY DISTRICT

receiving a job offer only to be undone by what they thought was a mi-nor dispute years ago that unexpectedly turns up on a police report. And candidates fail drug tests more often than one might expect. So I suggest that job candidates ensure that their "background" is positioned so that it does not sabotage their job campaign goals.

Indeed, what Mr. Tabone suggests here says it all!

AN EMPLOYMENT PROPOSAL

I will conclude this chapter and the book by introducing you to the concept of an employment proposal, yet another unique strategy for getting a job through a familiar, everyday sales and marketing practice. A universally accepted and expected sales approach is for sales professionals to present their products and services to prospective buyers and to provide a proposal (or a price) for those products and services. If you want your home painted, the painter provides you with a proposal. If you need a DJ for a wedding, the DJ provides you with a proposal. If you are purchasing a home or automobile, the sellers provide a proposal, or price, from which you can begin negotiations. In most cases, sellers provide proposals or prices to prospective buyers to initiate a positive transaction.

When selling yourself in a highly competitive job market, you are the sales professional. Prospective buyers, aka employers, are meeting with you to determine if you have "the goods" they want to purchase. This sales meeting, otherwise known as an interview, takes place. So here's a question to ponder. If you are the sales professional (job seeker) and are selling yourself to a would-be buyer (potential employer), why would you then wait for the buyer to make a proposal? In most other sales encounters the seller makes the proposal! *An employment proposal is a proactive, formal, written document submitted to a prospective employer offering your services and outlining a proposed employment arrangement. In the same way a business consultant would submit a proposal to a company for consulting services, you submit a proposal to a prospective employer for employment services!*

The employment proposal is highly effective especially when:

- You feel you might not be the strongest candidate for the job
- You know you are the strongest candidate for the job and want to take the initiative
- You were not offered the job or were rejected but still "have a chance"
- The hiring process has been delayed
- You want to propose that a company create a new job that does not currently exist but that would benefit the company
- You want to be considered as an independent contractor as opposed to an employee
- You want to stand out and be professionally aggressive

Make Them an Offer They Can't Refuse

The employment proposal is an innovative and effective method for demonstrating initiative. Drive and initiative are viewed favorably by most employers. They show you are an enterprising individual. In today's competitive job market, you must view yourself as self-employed and use every effective marketing tool to promote yourself to potential employers. An employment proposal is similar to any other proposal. It is an effective promotional instrument that communicates the distinct advantages you offer and the results you can deliver. Here is a sample employment proposal.

Melinda Grant

1234 8th Street • Freemont, MI 40002
(505) 555–6722 • email@email.com

March 14, 20__

Mr. James Allen, President
S.D. Allen & Company
9955 33rd Place
Freemont, MI 44403

Dear Mr. Allen:

Thank you for meeting with me yesterday. I thoroughly enjoyed meeting with you and your staff, touring your plant, and discussing the position of Accounts Receivable Manager. I am confident I can reduce your average outstanding accounts receivable from your present level of 68 days down to 32–35 days without compromising customer relations. This would free up over $200k in cash.

My Proposal:
There is no doubt in my mind that I can produce the results you want and work collaboratively with your staff. Furthermore, we share common values including professionalism, a strong work ethic, and providing extraordinary customer service in a team-spirited way. These values along with the value of "accountability" make me a good fit for your company.

I propose to you that I work for your company for a probationary period of 120 days. In that time, you can expect me to:

- Develop a credit policy that will improve customer relations and reduce A/R.
- Slash the average A/R aging from 68 days to 45 days in 120 days, with the goal of achieving 32–35 days within 6–9 months.
- Demonstrate that I have the skills and personality to warrant continued employment.

If, after 120 days, I have not met the goals or fit in with your culture, I will voluntarily resign, file no unemployment claim, and we part amicably. But I do not expect that to happen. You will see that I will be a valuable asset to your accounting department.

I would be willing to work at the lower end of the salary range that we discussed, secure in knowing that my performance will dictate future earnings. And I would be able to begin working on Monday, the 27th.

I hope you will give this proposal serious consideration, and I look forward to discussing this with you.

Sincerely,

Melinda Grant

CHAPTER 5 SUMMARY: BEST WAYS 81–101

81. Knowledge is not power. Knowledge is potential power. Power and success come from taking action on what you know. The fifth and final step of the five-step job transition process is that of taking action. Take massive action, implement your MAP, and you'll get massive results!

82. Take action and establish your campaign headquarters. Don't minimize the importance of having an inspiring place from which to conduct your job transition campaign.

83. Take action and dress to win! How you dress also determines the way you feel, your productivity, and your outcome. During the day, dress as if you will meet your next employer at any time.

84. Take action to eliminate obstacles to success. You must devote 100 percent of your resources and energy toward implementing your action plan to land a job in troubled job markets. So take the necessary action to avoid any distractions that will impair your campaign.

85. Take action to access technology. The Internet provides critical information in a timely manner that is necessary to land a job in any job market. You must gain access to a computer and know how to use it to optimize your campaign to quickly land a new job.

86. Take massive action and network to build your personal sales force. A good percentage of jobs are never advertised, or they are filled before they're advertised. More than ever, it's who you know and who you meet that will result in your next job, not what you know or how good you are.

87. Keep adding people to your network. When it comes to making new contacts and building new relationships, you can never have enough.

88. Get LinkedIn, and network online. Use Facebook and other social networking sites if your presence is strictly professional. Online networking is both highly enjoyable and very effective.

89. Do not ask people in your network for a job. By doing so, you place them in an uncomfortable position, and they'll avoid you from that point on. The networking process is one where you seek advice and information, not a job. You are looking for job leads or names of other people who might help you.

90. Take action to ace the interview. You must be as well prepared for the interview as presidential candidates are for their televised debates!

91. The interview is an equal encounter between two parties— one who has a position to fill and one who wishes to fill that position. Treat the interview as just a meeting. Although you shouldn't, by any means, treat this meeting lightly, you must keep in mind that there is a mutual need.

92. The key to acing the interview is to be well prepared. Prepare to convince the interviewer that you can do the job as well as or better than other candidates, and prepare to convince the interviewer that you're a good fit with the company.

93. You must know the company's needs. You need to know what the organization's problems are. You must know what the company's goals and objectives are. And then you need to blow your own horn confidently, not arrogantly, and convince the interviewers that you understand the company's needs.

94. While you are proving that you are qualified and capable of doing the job, you must also demonstrate to the interviewer that you are a good fit for the company or organization.

95. Arrive at the interview knowing the company's values and culture. In most cases, this information is easily accessible on the company's Web site. If, for instance, you know that a company's

values include honesty and integrity and going the extra mile to provide groundbreaking levels of customer service, you must communicate that you share these traits during the interview.

96. Be prepared to answer behavioral-based, or "case study," questions. A behavioral-based interview is made up of open-ended questions that ask you to illustrate and explain actual circumstances that you have previously faced.

97. Behavioral-based questions for candidates new to the job market, such as college graduates or first-time workers, may be hypothetical and "what-if" inquiries such as, "If this were to occur while on the job, how would you react?"

98. If the subject of salary comes up during the interview, the general rule is to try and avoid it until an offer has been made. This is because the greatest leverage you have is after the job offer but before acceptance.

99. Always mail or e-mail a thank-you note within hours following an interview. Unless you have a reason to do otherwise, keep the message short and subtly show your interest to move forward in the hiring process.

100. Be sure your references and "background" are in order so they don't sabotage your job campaign goals. What you don't know will hurt and prolong your campaign.

101. Consider using an employment proposal. An employment proposal is a proactive, formal, written document submitted to a prospective employer offering your services and outlining a proposed employment arrangement.

AUTHOR'S FINAL COMMENT

When I was fired by my one of my best friends back in 1992, there were five concepts my coaches taught me that made the most difference in helping me deal with, and overcome, my pain and disappointment. These concepts helped me identify a meaningful and exciting career when, at the time, I hadn't a clue what I wanted to do for a living at age 39. I would go so far as to say that these five ideas changed and actually saved my life. So I'll conclude by sharing with you these five concepts, knowing that if you embrace these messages, they will serve you as well as they have served me.

1. *I learned that it's not the wind that blows that really matters; rather, it's the set of the sail that makes all the difference.* I was taught that I can't control forces that I can't control. I can't control getting a lousy boss or getting fired. These things, my teachers taught me, are called the wind. But what I can control is the set of the sail, how I respond and react to the wind. When I realized that I alone control how I think and feel, no matter what the situation, I was able to achieve whatever I set my mind on achieving. The same holds true for you!

2. *I learned not to wish that things were easier; rather, that I was better.* I discovered that life is not about easy; it's about purpose, meaning, passion, love, contribution, sacrifice, and hard work. I discovered that life is about creating all that I can create in the short time that I'm on this planet. The same holds true for you!

3. *I learned that I am what I think; I am my thoughts.* I was taught to be the master of my own thoughts, because if I think I can do something, I will. And if I doubt I can do something, I won't. I learned that my thoughts are the blueprints for my future. The same is true for you!

4. *I learned that if I didn't plant in the spring, I'd have to beg in the fall.* I learned that with everything in life, including my career, I had to plant the seed of achievement so I could reap the rewards. I learned that I had to plant seeds of new ideas, new beliefs, and new commitments every day in order to find happiness and meaning in a new career and in my life. The same philosophy is true for you!

5. *Finally, I learned that I had to enjoy the journey in pursuit of the destination.* I have to admit, to this day, this remains one of my toughest challenges. But my teachers taught me that I have to be happy with what I have in pursuit of what I want. And yes, I discovered that true joy comes from living in the moment, enjoying the journey to the top. I discovered that every moment is a precious gift, because future moments are, in no way, guaranteed. The same is true for you!

And finally, beware of doubt. Never doubt yourself, who you are or the goals you are capable of achieving. Shakespeare said, "Our doubts are traitors and make us lose the good we oft might win, by fearing to attempt."

Thank you for spending this time with me.

INDEX

Achievements:
  adversity and, 19–21, 31–33
  in employment section of résumé,
    97–99
  impact of beliefs and thoughts on, 1, 7–8
  on value-based résumés, 81
Action, 8, 163–180
  background checks and, 174–175
  dressing to win, 164
  eliminating obstacles, 165
  employment proposals and, 175–177
  establishing job campaign headquarters,
    163–164
  importance of, 163
  interviews and, 168–174
  as Miracle Principle, 23
  personal sales force and, 166–168
  technology and, 165–166
  [*See also* Meticulous Action Plan
    (MAP)]
Adversity, conquering, 19–21, 31–33
Advisers:
  feedback on value-based résumés, 82
  in sphere of influence, 18–19
  (*See also* Networking)
All in the Family (TV program), 150
Alumni associations, 143
Attention, in focus management, 28
Attitudes (*see* Beliefs/thoughts)

Audience:
  confusing, 82
  in test-marketing résumés, 82
  for value-based résumés, 80, 82

Background checks, 174–175
Banister, Roger, 5–6
Behavioral-based interviews, 171–174
  nature of, 171–172
  tips for handling, 172–174
Beliefs/thoughts:
  changing, 2–4
  commitment and, 13, 16, 68
  controlling, 5–8
  desire for success, 16
  discipline, 17–18
  embracing adversity, 19–21, 31–33
  in empowering achievement, 1, 7–8
  about failure, 19–21, 31–33
  faith and, 16
  impact of, 1, 7–8
  importance of, 2, 4
  about landing a new job, 6–7
  in limiting achievement, 1, 7–8
  nature of, 3
  personal responsibility, 15
  power of, 5–6
  (*See also* Positive approach)
Best, Tim, 167

ABOUT THE AUTHOR

 **Jay Block** is an industry pioneer and one of the nation's leading executive career and empowerment coaches. He is the author of 15 career and motivational books, 10 of which are published by McGraw-Hill. Jay is a highly respected trainer and keynote presenter and is best known for combining world-class motivational techniques with cutting-edge job transitions tools and strategies. He has created four international certification programs and travels the country to share his ideas and concepts with job seekers and career trainers. Visit Jay at www.jayblock.com.

Crestwood Public
Library District
4955 W. 135th Street
Crestwood, IL 60445